Greensboro

Hillsboro

Bennett's
House

Raleigh

TO ~~RICHMOND~~

D0501418

NORTH

CAROLINA

Goldsboro

Fayetteville

New Bern

Cheraw

CAPE FEAR RIVER

PEE DEE

Florence

RIVER

Wilmington

CAROLINA

SANTEE RIVER

ATLANTIC
OCEAN

N
W E
S

Charleston

THE PATH OF
SHERMAN'S MARCH
TO THE SEA

Cottage Grove Public Library
700 E. Gibbs Ave
Cottage Grove OR 97424

0   Miles   100

0   Km   100

A CIVIL WAR COURTSHIP

OVERLEAF   *Edwin Weller, Orderly Sergeant, Company H, 107th New York Volunteers (1863)*

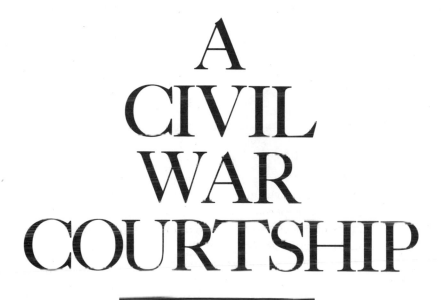

A CIVIL WAR COURTSHIP

The Letters of Edwin Weller
from Antietam to Atlanta

EDITED BY

WILLIAM WALTON

Doubleday & Company, Inc., Garden City, New York
1980

COTTAGE GROVE PUBLIC LIBRARY

Grateful acknowledgment is made to the National
Archives for permission to reproduce the photographs on pages 52–53, 172–73, and 192–93, and to
the Memorial Library, Montour Falls, New York,
for the photograph on pages 106–7.

Designed by LAURENCE ALEXANDER

ISBN: *0-385-15572-7*
Library of Congress Catalog Card Number
Copyright © 1980 by William Walton

ALL RIGHTS RESERVED
PRINTED IN THE UNITED STATES OF AMERICA
FIRST EDITION

A CIVIL WAR COURTSHIP

1

Another echo, faint but insistent.

The echoes of that war, more than a century ago, seem never to fade entirely away.

A twenty-three-year-old soldier writes home to the girl he left behind in an upstate New York village telling her about the war he is fighting.

There are few famous names in his letters and no new evidence of what happened at Gettysburg or Chancellorsville. But he was there and these were events in his life and as his letters pile up year after year they begin to sound like conversation, miraculously preserved, conversation that we now can overhear after all this time.

Battles emerge in their grisly horror and then dissolve into a rainstorm or a slow march onward across a new cornfield, another river, a tangled woodland. Everyday life goes on in between. The weather is more dominant than the enemy. There is poor food and cold wind, laughter and sadness. Talk of old friends back home and constant plans for a peaceable future. And there is love.

The conversation is all there as though it had been waiting for someone to listen.

The young soldier was one of thousands who fought at Antietam and Atlanta. Names of battles are remembered always, names of soldiers seldom.

His name was Edwin Weller. He learned a half-dozen ways to make hardtack edible, how to doctor blistered feet, and how to stalk an ingenious enemy—all because he believed President Lincoln when he said he needed help.

Edwin Weller had been clerking in a dry-goods store when the war began, a young man of limited wordly experience. The war brought him, in quick drafts, a lifetime of experience and more. As the new experiences pour in he begins in his letters to set things down, to describe newly captured cities and pretty girls glimpsed in passing, he mourns lost and wounded friends, sees southern gardens bursting into bloom and mud-soaked fields where he must bivouac for a cold, stormy night.

Constantly he longs for more news from home and to each incoming letter he responds eagerly, turning over every morsel of village news, savoring particularly the romantic gossip and speculating endlessly on whether matrimony will result.

Love and marriage, oddly enough, seem to be more on his mind than hate and warfare. At least he considers them more proper topics for correspondence.

The girl to whom he is writing, Antoinette Watkins—Nettie for short—seems at first to be anything but a romantic attachment. In his first letter he addresses her as "Friend Nett" and signs himself "very respectfully yours." Allowing for the customs and formality of the times, that is still anything but an ardent address. But as the letters stretch on through the war, new coloration slowly appears, a note of warmth, a teasing flirtatiousness, growing ardor, and finally grave, steady feeling. A bit stilted, yet never awkward, and always of transparent sincerity, his letters reveal a young man's passage from the boyishness of a new recruit into the manhood of a seasoned soldier, his emotions maturing with his experience in a grueling, bitter war.

In his first letter he boasts of a new mustache that will make the girls think he is "some foreign gentleman" when he comes home. He complains of recurrent toothaches and about the "constant marching and counter-marching" his regiment must do through northern Virginia.

And though anything but a master of English prose or spelling, he often manages to set the scene deftly. "As I sit here writing in the shade of a large oak tree," he wrote soon after Gettysburg, "I can still hear cannonading on the right." And later on from Georgia he reports that "bullets are flying over my head while I sit here on a hardtack box writing."

He has placed himself in a landscape and suddenly it seems perfectly credible that a tired soldier will write only a few paragraphs about a recent battle and then launch into detailed discussion of the ice-skating parties and sleigh rides and love affairs of Havana, New York, a faraway land of peace and innocent pleasures for which he pines.

Havana was a small town in south-central New York, two miles south of Watkins Glen and twenty north of Elmira. All of his regiment, the 107th New York Volunteers, had been recruited in that green, rolling country, and many were old friends, especially in Company H, which was made up almost exclusively of young men from Havana. In later years the town name was changed to Montour Falls, but in these letters it is still Havana and often referred to merely as "H."

Neither Edwin nor Nettie was a native of Havana. Nettie came from Oriskany Falls when her parents, Polly and Waterman Watkins, moved to Havana with their seven offspring, one son among six sisters of whom Nettie was the youngest.

Edwin, too, came of a sizable family. Born in 1839 in nearby Chemung County, he was a sixth-generation New Yorker. At the time of the Civil War his father, Theodore V. Weller, still lived there, and a few of the letters are addressed to him.

Naturally they have a different tone from the ones addressed to Nettie, more matter-of-fact, reporting on his health, his weight, and other things a parent would want to know.

And it was to his father that Edwin wrote quickly the very day after Gettysburg the good news that "the fatal bullett has again missed me."

To Nettie he wrote more discursively, describing the soldierly life and admitting that, to his own surprise, he liked it.

And even more surprising, that he seemed to be fitted for it.

"Going into battle," Edwin told her, he "thought of home, friends and everything else but as soon as we entered the woods where the shells and balls were flying thick and fast, I lost all fear."

That was soon after Antietam, where the 107th had first experienced combat and every one of the green, little-trained New York youths must have been asking himself the age-old question — am I a coward?

His attitudes toward "this bristly rebellion" are clearly defined, not with bitterness aimed at the Rebs firing at him from the woods but with stern disapproval of their leaders for disrupting the Union.

The great names of the war — Grant, Lee, McClellan, Hooker, Sherman — appear only in the luminous distance, even farther away than the mysterious higher echelons of brigade headquarters or corps or army. The common soldiers heard about those distant figures guiding their fates, but seldom saw them. Still they managed to form opinions of considerable validity — for instance, that Little Mac didn't seem to be the right leader for the Union forces, that Lincoln must be reelected, and that Sherman was worthy of a deep, abiding trust and faith in his generalship.

Sometimes Edwin struck a graver note with Nettie.

"Do not for a moment think or say that I may not return," he wrote her one night from Georgia. "I know such a thing is possible but I never allow myself to think of such a thing."

More often his tone was lighter, sometimes teasing her about a mysterious "Mr. Vail" who seems to have been pursuing Nettie, sometimes hinting that he too was seeking romantic companionship and any moment now might find a beautiful southern belle (usually spelled "bell").

And always he would come back to his fond memories of times together. "If I were sitting beside you on that old familiar sofa, and telling you in my usual way," he wrote from the South, and another time he recalls how he shook a peach tree while Nettie picked up the fruit and tried to keep him from eating it all.

What a pity Nettie's own letters to Edwin have not survived. All we can speculate is that they had enough sparkle and guile to make him long for more, year after year. And in the end, to achieve her goal.

At the time Nettie seems to have been living mostly with her sister and brother-in-law, Louise and Daniel Tracy, helping to rear their children and manage the household. Occasionally she visited two other married sisters living in Union Springs, at the northern end of Seneca Lake, where she performed similar family services, and from there kept up her correspondence.

Edwin's letters were preserved in the conventional family manner—in the attic—by his descendants, of whom I am one. When Nettie died in 1929, her daughter Helen Louise inherited the letters and stuffed them into a battered iron safe hidden under the curving staircase of our house in Illinois. After *her* death, my sister Helen Hackett became the owner of the old safe, magpie treasures and all.

Now I have unfolded those crumbly pages to learn something about the enigmatic bearded face always referred to as "your Grandfather Weller who fought in the Civil War."

As will be apparent, Edwin Weller was neither a grammarian nor much of a speller, but I have transcribed his words faithfully, even to letting him spell corps "corpse." The only emendations were made when he seemed to have dropped a word, perhaps in hasty writing, or when the absence of punctuation fogs the meaning. Otherwise the words and phrasing are all his.

Some letters have been shortened, largely when he rambled on about local gossip too long even for a devoted grandson to sustain attention. All excisions are indicated in the usual way.

2

In the summer of 1862, Edwin Weller's regiment, the 107th New York Volunteers, was recruited quickly in response to President Lincoln's appeal for 300,000 men to help put down "this unnecessary and injurious civil war."

The war was not going well for the Union. McClellan was trying again to take Richmond, this time by stripping northern Virginia of combat forces, transporting them by water, and launching his Peninsular Campaign from Yorktown, southeast of Richmond. Though McClellan engaged the main Confederate attention, Stonewall Jackson was, at the same time, rampaging up and down the Shenandoah Valley, making Lincoln extremely nervous that his capital might at any time be assaulted.

The first response to Lincoln's call was something less than enthusiastic, and that wily politician immediately started applying pressures to speed things along. Among his techniques was to call in key young congressmen and ask them to go back to their home districts as recruiters.

Working with Secretary of State Seward, himself a New Yorker, he summoned the representatives of the Elmira district which, because of a recent redistricting, had two members in the House, Alexander Diven and R. B. van Valkenberg. They hurried home at once, and twelve days after Lincoln's call, the first public meeting was held in Havana. Inevitably for those times, there was a Beecher present for the patriotic proceedings, this one the Reverend Thomas K. Beecher, Harriet Beecher Stowe's brother, who had left his Elmira pulpit to join the recruiting.

A week later Edwin Weller's name appears for the first time in the records of those exciting summer days. Four Havana men, including Weller, signed an appeal for enlistments published in the Havana *Journal*, and that same day he himself enlisted, and so became, as the regimental history later called him, the "first of the three hundred thousand."

The recruits were gathered in Elmira where private funds were raised to pay them quickly the bounties promised — twenty seven dollars from the federal government, fifty from the state. They were outfitted, given a few haphazard drills, and by August 14 they were off to war. The Elmira *Daily Press* reported the new regiment, accompanied by a civilian band hired from nearby town of Painted Post, "filled 25 cars" as the train headed for Washington.

And in Washington itself they were indeed all hailed as the first of the 300,000. President Lincoln and his Cabinet reviewed the regiment, and Secretary Seward gave them a new banner. Then, between dense crowds, they marched down historic Pennsylvania Avenue and across the Long Bridge into Virginia.

It was to be an incredible journey, through many states and many battles, before they marched again down the same avenue for the Grand Review when the rebellion had been put down. By then President Lincoln would not be there, but neither would many of these young recruits from upstate New York.

Edwin Weller was one of the lucky ones. And as the stifling August days went on, he wrote his first letter to the girl back home in Havana.

To Nettie Watkins
From Camp Seward, near Fort Lyon, Va.
August 26th, 1862

Friend Nett,

Having a few Spare moments, I thought I could not better improve them than by writing you a few lines. You have no doubt Heard all the details of our movements as far as our Camp near Washington, which Camp we left last Saturday morning and marched to this, our present Camping place. Our first Camp was a very plesant one, and well located but the one we have now I think far exceeds the other.

We are now located on the East Side of the Shennondoa Valley and about two miles South East of Alexandria and near Arlington Heights. We have a fine View of Washington and Georgetown Some ten miles North West of us and also Alexandria and the Potomac River. The River is only about a mile from us, So we get a good view of all Steamboats and Vessles passing up and down the River, which I assure you are not a few, for I can step out of my Tent most any time of day and See Eight or ten Steamboats and Vessles passing up or down. The Water here is very good for *this* State but is no Such Water as we got in York State.

There has been four Companies detailed from our Regiment to do Garrison duty in Fort Lyon. Our company is one of the four. Two companies went in this morning and we Expect to go in very Soon. McClellen's army is marching up the Valley to Reinforce Pope, already Forty Regiments have gone up and more are following. They are a pretty hard looking lot of fellows, they look as if they had Seen a great deal of Service.

There was a Rebel taken last Saturday night about two miles from here in the act of Poisoning a spring that another Regiment was using Water from. He was brought here to the Fort and put in Jail, it is thought he will be shot. It is now time for Dress Parade and I shall be obliged to defer writing till after Parade is over.

Six O'Clock, Parade is over and we are again through with another days drill. I tell you this Drilling is hard work, but it is what makes an effective Soldier, My Tent is Situated at the head of our Street, which is one of the plesantest ones in Camp. My Tent Mates are Second Sargt. G.M. Jackson formerly of Capt. Mulfords Company, and C.H. Duryea, Corporal, all other tents in Camp have five and six men in them.

Charley Duryea has been Sick for three or four days, but not so Sick that he had to go to the Hospitle. I Caught a very bad Cold night before last, and it Settled in My Teeth. I have a tooth ache ever Since.

I like Soldiering full as well as I expected to. I think if you could See me now you would laugh. I have got as black as any one *can* get in the short time I have been here. I tell you Nett I am raising a fine Mustach. Just wait till I go back to Havana. The people will think it is Some Foreign Gentleman.

Nett How does all the Young People flourish now, do you have your usual Set too's now days or rather nights. How I should like to be in Havana just *one* Night and have an old fashion time. Such as we use to have last Winter. You must excuse this hastily written letter and all mistakes for I have to Catch time to write between Drilling hours.

Remember me to all the young folks of Havana and tell

them all to write me. I shall Expect to hear from you Very Soon. I hope you will not fail to do So.

Very Respectfully Your Friend,
Edwin Weller

Direct to me
   In Care Capt. E.C. Clark
   107th Regt. N.Y.V.
   Washington, D.C.

P.S.   We can plainly hear the firing of Artillery today off South and I presume there is a battle being fought not far from us. According to reports there is Rebel guerrillas not but a short distance from us. I would not be surprised if we had a skermish before long. Nothing more this time.

Respectfully, Edd

After this first letter there is a gap. No letter has survived from the crucial two months when Edwin Weller and the 107th received their baptism of fire in the bloody Battle of Antietam, September 17, 1862.

Perhaps events were too swift and too strange for him to record, particularly since he had not yet settled into the rhythm of regular letter writing, a practice that stayed with him for the rest of the war.

Later on he also kept a diary, largely a record of weather and routine events, seldom describing military action and never alluding to thoughts or feelings. Only during the period of Sherman's March to the Sea have I found the diary worth quoting, as will be seen.

To fill the gap between late August and November, when he
again takes up the story, the best source of information is the
History of the 107th N. Y. Volunteers, replete with detailed first-
person accounts written soon after the war. In addition, the Elmira and Havana newspapers in the next few decades gave
generous space to regimental reunions when the veterans gathered to reminisce, refight old battles, and crack old jokes.

Ten days after Edwin's first letter his regiment received the
expected marching orders to follow other troops already
streaming northward where Rebel forces seemed to be heading.
Historians have determined that Lee's over-all plan was to in-
vade Maryland and bring that border state into the Confederacy, thus isolating Washington and opening rich, heavily popu-
lated Pennsylvania to invasion — all of which might encourage
European governments to recognize the Confederacy.

On a moonlit night, September 6, the new recruits from
New York shouldered arms at Camp Seward and headed toward the Aqueduct Bridge over the Potomac. One marcher
remembered later that just as the dark mass of men and
wagons reached the Georgetown side, someone started singing
"The Battle Hymn of the Republic" and soon the stirring song
had caught on down the line, company to company, until this
great mass of moving men were singing "We are coming, we
are coming 300,000 strong."

He also observed that this was the last time they *all* marched
together.

The night of September 16 found the 107th spread through
a dew-wet clover field at Antietam, Maryland, facing Rebel-
held woodlands, no singing now, the silence broken only by an
occasional picket shot.

The next day's battle has been called "the bloodiest single
day's fighting of the Civil War." The 107th was committed to
action at the middle of the Union lines near a cornfield and a
small Dunker church which that day achieved immortality.

The commander of Company H (from Havana) wrote later:

"I shall never forget how your company looked as I took Orderly Weller's report a minute or so before our introduction to the first shell which fortunately did not explode."

Though the 107th was used that day only as a support force, never as a front-line element, casualties were heavy. The first man fell dead as they moved across a plowed field to a wooded area, and when darkness ended the battle, nearly two hundred men of the regiment were dead or gravely wounded.

Next day the Southerners retreated slowly back across the Upper Potomac, and the 107th, with other units, was posted at Maryland Heights, guarding the crossing. Through October the regiment, buffeted by bad weather and insanitary conditions, suffered further heavy casualties as illness swept the camp. Finally they were moved back to Antietam Ford, a better site, and from there Edwin's letters to Nettie resume.

To Netty Watkins
From Camp near *Antietam Ford, Md.*
November 21st, 1862

Dear Friend Nett,

Yours of the 26th of Oct. was received Some three weeks ago. I should have answered it long ere this had my Duties permited, but it Seems that every thing has had to be done and no one but myself to do it, but never mind, there is a better day a coming. I was very glad indeed to hear from you. Also to hear that you were enjoying yourself So well. Of course, the return of the Band, and especially a certain *one* of it, would be *cause* for joy. I have heard from both of my Brothers Several times. They are glad to be back home, how I should like to See them.

I think by your tell, you must have had pretty gay times while the Institute was in Session. I should like to have been one among you, but you would not caught me going after Grapes for you know it is against my principals to do anything of the Kind. But Still I should like to had a few of the Grapes to eat. How Soon do you think the talked of "Social Hops" will commence. I hope you will be favored with a few Hops this Winter So as to Keep in practice for I want to have one good old Dance when I get out of this War. If there Should be a Scarcity of Young men just drop me a line some day, and I will come down and attend one Hop to fill up. How I should like to have witnessed that reunion you Spoke of in your letter. No I will take that back, for I should not. It would have been *to much* for my Young and tender heart, Especially when I am So deeply concerned. . . .

We heard yesterday for the first time Since he was taken from Lieut. L.O. Sayler, he has been Paroled and is at the Camp of Paroled Prisoners at Annapolis waiting to be exchanged. We moved from Maryland Heights a little over three weeks ago to this place. We have now one of the plesantest camps that we have ever occupied. This is Said to be our Winter Quarters. We have been at Work for two weeks building Log Huts for Winter. I finished mine about a week ago. It is called the best one in Camp. I talk very strongly of marrying and settling down in it for the Winter. There is Said to be Some very gay young Ladies not more than a mile from Camp, and I think I know of one in camp and who do you suppose it is, it is the celebrated Nett Heill. She looks as natural as ever, and I should judge as gay. I thought my eyes deceived me when I saw her but I found it was reality. I do not know how long she intends to Stay, but

I presume Some time. She arrived here yesterday with another lady, the Wife of one of the Soldiers.

We are Stationed here for the purpose of guarding the Ford across the Potomac. It is considered quite an important point. We Send out Picket to guard it every day. This Picket duty is pretty tough business in this Cold, rainey and muddy weather but thank fortune I do not have to Stand Picket. An Orderly is exempt from all such duties. Rebels have been Seen on the oposite Side of the River on Several occasions but in no great numbers.

Enclosed you will find the card of our 1st Lieut. Donnolly. He Saw who I was writing to, and having Seen you Several times and never having an introduction thought he would Send you his Card, but Cards being a Scarce thing in the army put his name on a Sheet of Note, as you will See. Donnolly is a fine fellow, and pretty gay. Him and I have had Some pretty gay times together. He is one of my best friends. Now Nett here is a pretty good Chance for you. I think you must have made quite an impression. I do not think of anything more of importance to write So I will Stop this Scribbling. You will do well if you can read it. . . .

Very Respectfully Your Friend
Edwin Weller

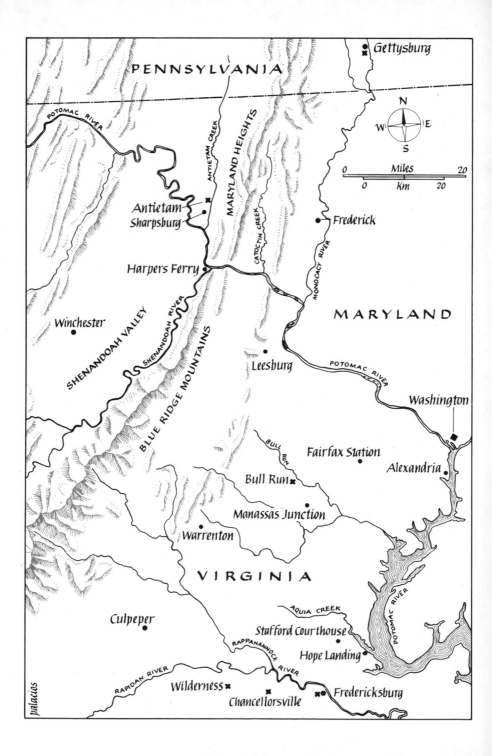

To Nettie Watkins
From Camp Near *Fairfax Station, Va.*
January 6th, 1863

Dear Friend Nett,

Your Very welcome letter of the 7th of Dec. was received about two weeks ago and I should have answered it long before this had it not been for our marching and counter-marching all over the State of Virginia. We have now got Settled again for a Short time I hope, and possible but not probably, for all winter.

Our Camp is located about half a mile from the Station in a piece of Woods. We have been at work for a week past building Log Huts to make us Comfortable. We have about half of them finished. I have Succeeded in getting one built for myself and a very comfortable one too. It is about as large as Molly Walkers front room, with a good Fireplace in it. Two nice Bunks and a Stationary Table built up on one Side, and Stools around it, these with other little conveniences make it quite Comfortable.

It is raining quite hard today. I think the annual rainy Season of this Section is now commencing. If So we shall have three or four weeks rainy weather here. I will give you a Short Sketch of our march from Antietam Md. We Started from Antietam Ford on the 10th of Dec. and marched toward Harpers Ferry about five miles and Bivouaced for the night, the next morning arose at half past three got our Breakfast and Started on our march at half past four, arrived at Harpers Ferry at about Eight O'Clock, halted there Nearly half an hour then marched through town and across the River (Potomac) on a Pontoon Bridge

Battlegrounds Near Washington

into Loudon Valley and down the Valley Five miles and Bivouaced for the night in an open field. The night was very cold and the only way we could Keep Warm was to build up a good large Fire and Sit or Wrap ourselves up in our Blankets and lay down beside it.

The next day arose Early got our Breakfast and marched through Hillsborough and beyond three or four miles when our advance Guard came upon a Party of Whites Rebel Guerrilla Cavellerymen. They had succeeded in Capturing some of our Baggage Wagons and one of our Sutters Wagons loaded with Supplies which were in the advance. Gen'l Williams Sent a party of our Cavellerymen in persuit of them, they overhauled them a Short distance to the Right of us and recaptured the Wagons and also a few Prisioners they took with the Wagons. We then marched on Encamping that night near Leesburgh.

The next day marched through Leesburgh (which is a regular Rebels nest in my opinion) and to within a few miles of Centreville and Bivouaced for the night. That Day we marched between Twenty and Thirty miles and when night came my feet was blistered nearly all over So that in fifteen minutes after we halted I could hardly walk a step but on taking Some salt and Water and bathing my feet throughly and then applying Liquor I managed to get myself in tolerable good marching order for the next day. The next day, Sunday, arrived here and encamped over night. The next morning marched out to and crossed the Occoquan River and toward Dumfries Eight miles.

We remained in this vicinity for two days awaiting orders but at the End of the two days Recvd. orders to march back to this Station which we did. We remained here nearly a week before we were called upon to march again. Then we were Sent out to and crossed the Occoquan River in a

reconnoissance but found no enemy except a few Cavellerymen which we dispersed in Short order. While we were out
a Party of Rebel Cavellerymen attempted to get to this Station but were repulsed by a small force which was left
behind to Guard the Station. They Succeeded however in
getting to the RailRoad above and below the Station and
tearing up Some of the Track. It was repaired and in runing
order by that night when we returned to our Camp.

It is thought by Some that we may be Sent nearer to
Washington but it is hard telling where we Shall go or how
long we may remain in one place. The 141st Regt. is encamped about Twelve miles from us at Miness Hill. I received a letter from Chas. Durkee a few days ago. He is well
and seems to like the Service. But I will Stop this Kind of
War Trash.

I was very much Surprised to hear that certain young
ladies of Havana Should be guilty of making So much noise
in Sunday School. Had I been there I certainly should have
brought them to Silence. I received a letter from the Rev.
Mr. Chester a few days ago Saying that he had Sent me
Some Books to distribute in our Regiment. I concluded
these must be the Books that the collection was taken up for
in your Sabbath School. The books however have not come
to hand yet as we have recvd. no express matter Since we
came here but think it will come Soon or be ordered
forward.

You Say Nett you have often wondered what a persons
feelings or thoughts were when they were going into Battle.
I can not Speak for others but I can tell you how I felt.
When we first Started from our position as a reserve to the
Woods near where the Rebels were, I thought of Home,
friends, and most everything else, but as Soon as we Entered the Woods where the Shells and Balls were flying

thick and fast I lost all fear and thought of Home and friends, and a Reckless don't care disposition Seemed to take possession of me. Then was two of our Company Shot down near me and Even their Shrieks and yells did not affect me in the least. This is the way I felt and I have heard other Soldiers Say the Same. . . .

I see by the latest Havana Journal that has been received in Camp, that S.C. Keller and Octave H. have at last joined hands in Holy Wedlock. Success to them and may their many efforts be crowned with plentifullness and Peace. I can hardly Say as I envy Sam in but one respect and that I will not name, I leave you to judge. I am looking forward to the days when I may pay my distresses to Some fair Widow lady made So by this terrible War. The Widows must of course be attended to first you Know.

I handed Leuit. Donnelly the note enclosed, in your letter to me, and I presume you have heard from it long before this. I assure you it was refreshing to look upon your lovely countenance once more. I was not expecting to receive So nice a present, but I assure you I shall take the best care of it. Yours is the only Photograph or Picture of any Kind that I have here with me, and you certainly deserve Considerable credit for Sending me this. How I should like to be in Havana a few days to Skate and take a few Sleigh rides with you young Folks.

I will bring this hastily written letter to a close hoping you will excuse all errors in writing or otherwise. Answer Soon and Give me all the news of the day in Havana. . . .

Very Respectfully, Your True Friend
Edwin Weller
Direct all letters to Washington

To Theodore V. Weller Esq.
Niles Valley P.O.
Tioga County, Pa.
Politeness Capt. H.M. Slocum (on envelope)

From — Camp of 107th Regt.
    Near *Fairfax Station, Va.*
    Jany. *17th 1863*

Dear Father,

As I have an opportunity of Sending a letter I improve the opportunity. We have marching orders and will leave here tomorrow morning early, unless the order is countermanded which I think will not be done. We know nothing of our destination as usual, but imagin that we are going toward Richmond.

I am enjoying good health and weigh more than ever before. I was weighed two or three days ago and weighed 161 lbs. This is a good weight for me. You have probably Sent my Box before this, but it has not yet come to hand. I have at least two and I think three boxes or Packages on the way. I have received notice that there was a Package at Alexandria for me but could not get it forwarded to me as the R.R. running to this place is a Government R.R. and will not bring anything up unless ordered by the commander of the Brigade.

The weather is quite cold here today, and growing colder. Yesterday and today have been the coldest days I have Seen Since I came South. It will be pretty tough to lay out in Such Cold Weather but Such is a Soldiers life, *Rough.* There was four men belonging to our company Deserted last night. This makes 12 in all that had Deserted our com-

COTTAGE GROVE PUBLIC LIBRARY

pany. We have Twenty-Six in Hospitals. This leaves our Co. with but 49 Enlisted men now. When we left Elmira we had 98 Enlisted men and three commissioned officers. Now we have but one Commissioned officer and 49 Enlisted men — quite a difference. It has now been three weeks Since I have received a letter from you So I shall Expect another Soon. If Soldiers friends Knew how anxious they were to hear from home I think they would write oftener. We are ordered to Send all our Sick to Alexandria to the Hospital — we shall send three from our company.

I suppose Mary [his sister] has gone back to Elmira before this, has she not? Has Helen [another sister] returned Home from Millport yet. I hear that the old Pine Valley Bridge has burned down. This must have detained the Trains Some time. I recvd. a letter from D. Tracy a few days ago, he Says business is better with him than ever before.

There has been no appointments of Lieuts. made in our Company yet — and I do not Know as Diven will ever get it done, he is Slower than time.

I cannot think of much to write as I have So many Co. matters to attend to between now and morning that my mind is fully occupied. I have also my own things to pack yet tonight. So good night — write soon as you can. My love to all.

Your Affect. Son
Edwin

To Nettie Watkins
From Bivouac Near *Hope Landing, Va.*
January 31st, 1863

Dear Friend Nett,
    Your Very welcome letter of 25th Inst. was received Yesterday and I hasten to answer. It is Seldom that I answer a letter So Soon, but today having a few spare moments I thought I could not better improve them than by writing *you* a letter. A Soldiers correspondence, and the hearing from his old associates and friends is one of the greatest consolations he has in this Army, at least it is So with me.
    It does me a great deal of good to hear from my friends in Havana. I received a letter from Grove this morning giving me all the news. I am indeed glad to hear that the Young People of H. are so lively this Winter and enjoying themselves in various ways. I only wish I could be there to enjoy Some of your Parties with you. I think I could appreciate a Party like that at Reading Centre or at the Montour House.
    We left Fairfax Station on the morning of the 19th Inst. Marching through Dumfries and Aquia, we also crossed the Occoquan River on our March. The first two Days the Roads were in good condition to march, but the night of the Second it commenced raining and continued all night. The next morning we arose early got our Breakfast in the rain, ate and started on our march.
    We soon came to Dumfries Creek which had Swollen Very much during the night taking away the bridge over the Stream. We threw across a few Trees and part of the Regiment crossed on them, but the water rose So fast that it Soon became impossible for us to cross as Some of the last ones that tryed to cross fell in the Stream and came very near drowning. Then we went at work and built a Bridge

across, and Soon were all across Safe. The mud was So deep
that we were not able to march but three miles that day, as
we are never allowed to march any faster than the Artillery
and Baggage Train can move. We were five days in marching Forty-five miles, but if the roads had been good we
should have marched it in two.

Nearly every night we were obliged to put up our little
"Dog Shanties" as we call them, on the damp or rather *wet*
ground. Many is the sleepless night I have passed in this
way. All this I *freely* do, if by So doing I can aid in quelling
this bristly rebellion. When we first came here we encamped near Stafford Court House for three days where we
received Pay for three months. We were then detailed to
Come to this landing to Repair Roads So that supplies can
be got up to "Sugals" *Grand Army Corpse* which is encamped
at the Court House and to which our Regiment belong. We
do not expect to remain here but a few days then we expect
to go back to the C.H. to encamp again.

Since we arrived here we have experienced a severe
Snow Storm lasting Two Days, nearly covering up our little Shanties of Cloth but the last two days have been So
Warm that it has nearly all disapeared making the mud
much deeper than it was before. It will now be impossible
for the Army of the Potomac to make a forward movement
— short of Five or Six weeks. This will give us quite a rest
again.

The next day after we arrived at the C.H. I was very
agreeable Surprised at receiving a visit from our old friend
Miner Broderick who is detached from his Company and
now with the Signal Corpse, which when we came here
belonged to "Sugals" Corpse, but has Since been attached
to our (Slocums) corpse. Since then Miner has been to See
me nearly every day until we came here and he has been

here once and stayed with me all day. Miner is looking first rate and Sayes he is Enjoying the best of health. He is the Same old Miner yet. He wished to be remembered to you.

I am sorry to hear of Ed Clauhertys misfortune. It is indeed a Sad thing for as young a man as he, but Such is the Fortune of War. This deserting him for Doc Wells as Frank T. has done makes his Situation more Sad I presume and I Sympathise with him much, but Still it is no more than I should expect of her. If it were me I should just tell her to go to —— I will not tell you where but I tell you the best way to get along, and that is to never have any particular one Selected as a favorite unless he has Serious intentions. And, as you Say, what makes the matter much worse is her deserting a "Brave Soldier Boy," for a civilian. The "Soldier Boy" Should be first in the Ladies Estimation, of Course. These Soldier Boys are great Institutions I suppose, at least the Ladies should think So.

You speak of our Visit up to Kate Mix just before I left. Yes, indeed we did have a splendid time that Evening and I *often* think of those plesant times I have had with the Young People of Havana. You ask if I have any nice looking Gentlemen Friends here in the Army who would like to place their Photographs in a nice Young ladies hands. I presume there is lots of them that would like the chance but Nett, Photographs are entirely out of the question here, I do not think there is hardly a young man in our Regiment that has a Photograph of himself with him. I have no doubt but most of them have the Picture of the "Girls they left behind them." I should be pleased to aid you in filling up your Album with nice Pictures, and will do so if I have an opportunity for I think they could not place their Photographs in better hands than yours. . . .

In regard to my prospects of a Lieutenency I will tell you.

My name has been Sent in for a Commission as Second
Lieut. of our Company and one of our Sergeants by the
name of Whiteham has been recommended as 1st and Lieut
Donnelly as Captain. So you can See there has been more
wire pulling in our Company again. Similar to that at Elmira when our first lot of officers were elected. I will tell
you more about it Some other time and give the full details.
Chas. Duryea is well and Send lots of love. . . . I shall try to
go to Washington as Soon as I receive my commission
(which I am expecting every day) to get my outfit. The
greatest hindrance will be in getting a pass. Where we are
now encamped we have a fine View of the Potomac and
Aquia Creek also of Aquia Creek Landing and the Shipping
around there, forming the Blockade.

I think it about time to close this Scribbling for I think
you will do well if you can read what I have written. Please
remember me to Mr. and Mrs. Tracy and family and
especially to little Sarah [her niece]. Also remember me to
all the Young People. Now Nett if you will follow my good
example in answering so Soon I shall be paid for answering
you So Soon as I have.

Very Respectfully Your *Sincere Friend*
and Well wisher

Edwin Weller

To Netty Watkins
From Camp of 107th Regt. N.Y. Vols.
Near *Hope Landing, Va.*
March 15th, 1863

Dear Friend Nett,

Your long expected letter came to hand three or four days Since. I had thought I would wait as long before I answered as you did but when I took the Second thought I came to the conclusion that I had no good excuse for doing So and that I would not be living up to the instructions of the Good Book which Sayes we should always return good for evil. And then you did not wish me to retaliate by waiting So long as you had. Consequently in accordance with your wish I improve my first opportunity to answer. I am enjoying the best of health at present and am fat as a Pig.

I was glad to hear that you were all having such splendid times in Havana. I hope you may always enjoy yourself as well. I very often think of all my old associates in H. and wish that I might be among you for a few days to enjoy Some of your Sociables and with you, but I am, as you Say, a Soldier Boy and my place is here with my Regt. and Co. to do my Countries Service.

I am perfectly contented here, have lotts of fun in Camp every day. I like camp life but can't say that I like marching and fighting. There is Something about Soldiering that is romantic and a great many get So much accustomed to the life that they like no other. I sometimes think that if I was to go home now to remain I should not be contented, would probably want to go in the Service again, but if I ever get a chance, and can get a Furlough for a few days I shall try home I think. . . .

Today it is awful cold here. No snow on the ground but it has just commenced Hailing. We have had two or three days of very cold weather within the last week. Colder than we had in the Winter. I do not mind it much as I am pretty comfortably situated in a good Log shanty with a good fireplace near which I am now writing.

You ask me if I do not wish this War would close and I could be placed back in my old position in D. Tracys store. Indeed I do Nett, for it would be for the good of the country to have this Horrible war closed, and I have no doubt but that I should like it better in a short time, for I should enjoy more real Solid enjoyments and could choose my own Society, but not so in the Army. I have to associate with all classes here. . . .

Nett I have become a model cook Since entering the Army, and I think you will agree with me when I tell you how many kinds of dishes I can make out of Hardtack, 1st make Pancakes out of them, 2nd Hoecake, 3rd Flour Gravy, 4th Sause, 5th Coffee, 6th, Fry them. Of late we have drawn Flour and Soft Bread. The Flour we make Biscuit and Pancakes of. I think I can beat the natives making Wheat Pancakes. I get them as light and nice as you please and we think they make pretty good eating. But the hardest of it is we have to pay 60¢ per pound for all the Butter we get. This makes it pretty high living for a Soldier.

I think what I have written about my knowledge of cooking a pretty good Advertisement if it was generally Known by the Young ladies of my acquaintance. I am confident That my market would Soon be made, and I am not sure but that I had better put an advertisement in the Havana Journal stating my case. What think you? But hold, my friends down town have got that matter all arranged So I shall have no further trouble about it and do not need to advertise. How fortunate I am. Such a terrible burden taken off my shoulders. . . .

Capt. D. when he returned brought me some delicacies sent me by Mrs. Hull Fantin. They were very nice indeed. I have writen to Mr. P. Tracy today and tendered my many thanks for their Kind remembrance of me. I also received two pairs of nice Woolen Socks sent me by Mr. D. Tracy for which give him my thanks. Well, I think I have spun out a pretty long yarn so I will close. Remember me to Mr. Tracy's family and all who may enquire after me. How I should like to be at I I. and walk down to Church with you tonight. It would be a great pleasure. Now Nett, I shall expect you to answer Soon, please do So.

And believe me ever Your Friend,
Edwin Weller
Co. H., 107th N.Y.

To Theodore Weller
From Camp of 107th Regt N.Y. Vols.
Hope Landing, Aquia Creek, Va.
March 29th, 1863

Dear Father,

Your letter of the 22nd Inst. was received yesterday and I hasten to answer. I am enjoying good health at present. Yesterday we had another very hard rain storm which makes the roads much worse than before. This will delay a forward movement full a week. I think however there will be an advance within two weeks. I used to think when at the North that I knew what muddy roads was, but they do not compare at all with the roads here, at this time of the year.

There is but little doubt but that we have got a pretty active campaign before us this Spring and Summer and much
hard fighting will be done. The Rebels will of course make a
desperate resistence but I think the Government is fully determined to push this war through as fast as possible and
end it. I hope it will be done for this thing has run long
enough.

We were all glad when we heard of the passage of the
Conscript Law and only hope they will enforce it. Let a lot
of those home guards, as we call them, comedown here and
go through what we have and they will not croak quite so
much about the Army and why it does not do more. I am of
the opinion if we had about fifty or one hundred thousand
more troops we could end this thing in about three months
more, but we probably shall not get them as soon as that.

I have entirely given up getting a commission. When Col.
Diven was in Washington I wrote to him inquiring if I had
really been recommended for a position and when Capt.
Donnelly returned from home he stopped in Washington
two days and saw Diven, he told Donnelly to tell me that
my name had been sent in and that my commission ought
to have come to me before that. Well, I said no more about it
then, but Diven returned to the Regt. in about a week from
that time and two or three days after one of our line officers
told me that a 2nd Lieut, from Elmira Co. had been recommended for 1st and Whiteham of our Co. for 2nd Lieut.
This of course leaves me in the background.

I hardly know what to think of Diven. If this be true, he
is nothing but a snake in the grass, that is my opinion of
him. As soon as I learned this news I immediately wrote to
Cook who is in Albany asking it as a favor that he would see
to the matter for me. There has nothing been heard of the
matter since, so I do not know how it will come out, but

there is one thing certain, and that is if I get a position I shall not be indebted to any one in this Regt. for it. I should like to have visited you this spring if I could get away but it will be impossible now I think as a forward movement will soon commence.

The stamps you sent me came all O.K. What does Leroy intend to go into this summer. Uncle ought to try and get him a good situation in Elmira, or some other place. Enclosed I send you a letter of mine that was published in the American Presbyterian and Evangelist, printed in Philadelphia. Some two months ago I received a letter from the Rev. Mr. Chester of Havana stating that the Presbyterian Sabbath School had sent me a package of books called the Soldiers Friend for distributing. In two or three weeks the books arrived and I distributed them as directed. Chester also wished me to write a letter discribing how the books were received etc. and direct it to the Sunday school. I did so and day before yesterday Adjt. Fantin returned from a visit home and brought me the Paper containing the letter, then told me that I was getting very notorious up North from letters I wrote to friends there. This is the first I knew anything about this letter's being published. I did not write it thinking that they would publish it, and provoked that it was allowed to be published, but there is one good thing about it my name is left out. I have heard from the letter through friends there before and what was thought of it, but did not dream they would have it put in the papers. I shall be careful what kind of letters I write after this if they are to pass around. I do not think of anything more of importance now. Give my love to all the folks and write soon

Edwin

To Netty Watkins
From Camp of 107th Regt. N.Y. Vols.
Near *Hope Landing, Va.*
April 8th, 1863

Dear Friend Nett,
   Your letter of 30th Mch. came to hand two or three days
ago. It is indeed a great pleasure to receive and peruse a
letter from you. It makes one think of bygone days so
plesantly spent in your company. I was glad to receive So
promt a reply to my last epistle. Promtness is indeed a Vir-
tue. This is necessary for a Correspondent to be fully appreciated. I would not give a fig for a correspondent that delays
weeks and Somtimes months before answering my letters.
One of the greatest conforts of a Soldier is his letters received from promt friends.
   I was a little Surprised when I first recvd. your letter
Postmarked Union Springs and for a moment thought I did
not Know who my Correspondent was but in a Second
glance at the handwriting I made up my mind that it was
from my fair friend Miss N.W. I should have recognized the
hand writing much Sooner probably if the title of Lieut.
had not been prefixed to my name which title I am not yet
authorized to attach to it as I have not been appointed yet
and probably will not be for Some time yet. . . .
   Speaking of my coming home on a Furlough, Nett. It is
almost impossible for me to get home now I have So much
to occupy my time. Capt. D. has been quite unwell for
nearly a week and I have had all the Company matters to attend to, but if we should stay here a few weeks longer I shall

Antoinette Watkins (1864)

make an application for a few days leave. Nothing could better please me than to go home for two or three weeks this Spring. I could enjoy myself finely. I should then, as you Say, live over Some of my old gay times I have had in Havana.

I hear that most of the N.Y. 3rd are reinlisting for two years. Do you think Charly will reinlist? Please give my best Respects when you write him again. Yes, I have great reasons to be very happy over my success and the complete Settlement of all my future prospects. I am extremely happy and almost begin to think it true, it has come very near Sending me up Several times, but I hear they have lately settled down to the fact that they Know nothing about the matter, which I think nearer the truth than any-thing they have Said very lately. Of course I have told Some of my friends that I Considered myself very happy, and intended to go home Soon as possible and take to myself a better half. For Some time two or three of my friends were in quite a query to Know who the young lady was. Some of them made guesses at the name of the lady, but could not Settle down on any particular one. Most every Young lady in H. being named. . . .

I am often reminded of many plesant times and little frol-ics I have had taking a look at your Photograph which by the way is a good picture of you. As good a one as I ever Saw I think. I assure you it is refreshing to gaze upon your lovely countenance every two or three days and Sometimes oftener. Yours is the only ladies Photograph I have with me, and I prize it very much for it always reminds me of Some of my happiest days.

I presume if I should come home now you would hardly know me. Geo. Courin was down here Some three or four weeks ago and thought I had changed very much. Of course

I do not notice it as much as others. I took tough now. But I must Stop for it is Supper time and I must go to work at Cooking. I have writen Everything in the way of nonsense I could think of so I will close. Remember me to Daniel and Wife also the children and all other who may enquire. Write me soon.

P.S. Duryea Sends Regards, he has been promoted to a Sargeant of our Co.

> As Ever Your Friend
> Edwin Weller
> 1st Sergt. Co. H.
> 107th N.Y. Vols.
> Washington D.C.

Thurs. eve.

Today we buried another of our comrads who died yesterday, his name is Andrew Devitt from Hecter. This makes the fourth man we have lost Since coming here. Grove tells me that Doc Grannis has gone home to Stay. Do you hear from him. Please Remember me to him when you write him. We go to Stafford C.H. tomorrow morning to be reviewed by Genls. Slocum and Williams and President Lincoln. I shall probably See Miner Broderick there, he is down to See us most every week. He is a gay chap I tell you. No more this time.

> Yours for ever and ever
> Ed.

Lincoln reviewed the troops April 10 and managed to increase their admiration for him. He arrived on a fine horse escorted by lancers, their red guidons fluttering in the Spring breeze. Lincoln's horsemanship impressed his soldiers, who remembered, in their regimental history, how he cantered onto the field and dashed up and down the spick-and-span lines of soldiers faster than his escort.

Mrs. Lincoln and other ladies sat in carriages also guarded by lancers, and when the President joined them for the pass-by, his black-clad figure, topped by a tall stovepipe hat, loomed larger than any other in the sparkling scene.

Northern Virginia was packed with troops that spring as the war's third summer approached, a season both sides hoped would be decisive. They were, of course, to be disappointed, especially in the war-weary North.

3

Both North and South were desperately in need of a victory. Four times the North had tried to take Richmond and each time failed, the most recent in December, shaking the morale of the Army of the Potomac.

The South's needs were no less critical. Grant was threatening Vicksburg to win control of the Mississippi and split the Confederacy. The loss at Antietam had dimmed Confederate hopes of foreign recognition and help. Both manpower and supplies were becoming critical.

All of northeastern Virginia was a crowded war theater where Lee and Hooker matched their unequal talents in devising strategies to achieve clear-cut victory, not merely movement. In weeks of fighting, Lee came closest, with a vast plan military analysts deem his masterpiece. In the climax at Chancellorsville, Union losses far outstripped those of the Confederates.

Masterpiece or not, the view from inside the vast battle scene was foggier than on the generals' maps. A few days afterward Edwin Weller, writing to his father, recorded one man's intimate view.

From Camp of the 107th N.Y. Vols.
Stafford Court House, Va.
May 8th, 1863

Dear Father,

You are no doubt quite anxious to hear from me since our late very active and fatiguing operations. Consequently I improve the few spare minutes I have to scribble you a few lines.

We left Hope Landing the 26th of April and joined our brigade at this place. 27th commenced our march to Kellys Ford on the Rappahannock River, crossed at the Ford the 29th marched to the Rappadan River where we came upon a detachment of Rebels building a bridge across the river. We attacked them, capturing 103 & killing one. The detachment numbered 125 the rest escaped.

As the bridge was not finished we were obliged to wade the river and the water being about 3 1/2 feet deep. We bivouaced on the opposite side for the night. Next morning resumed our march. That day the 30th reached Chancellorsville Forks where we had a small skirmish with the Rebs.

The most of the next day (1st inst.) was occupied in taking position and entrenching ourselves with ———— [indecipherable] and then skirmishing through the day. By noon the next day (2nd) we had our lines of entrenchments completed and toward night the Ball opened. The enemy attacked us on our left and worked gradually toward our right. When they got about the center opposite where we were entrenched they fell back a little, and we were ordered out of our entrenchments to push them still farther back. At the same time they threw a heavy force around to our right and drove our troops from their works. The 11th Corps held the entrenchments on the right. This of course created some confusion and our Corps (12th) fell back to *our* entrenchments. At night the battle ceased.

The next morning it commenced again and we were obliged to fall back to a better position. Before falling back however our brigade engaged the enemy and repulsed one brigade of the Rebs and would have done the same to a second brigade of them if we had not got out of amunition and were relieved by another brigade and left the field.

We were under very heavy fire while in but did good execution. It is said we were the only brigade that repulsed the Rebbles that day. We lost in our regt. 6 killed and 85 wounded and missing, from our co. only three wounded and 2 missing.

The battle goes far ahead, I think, of the one at Antietam in violence. The 107th stood right to the spot and gets considerable praise for its pluck.

Col. D—— had his sword shot from him by a shell. He was very cool and stood right up to the task during the engagement. The 6th we recrossed the river and returned to this place.

We are now under marching orders again and expect to move within two or three days, but we know not where to. I cannot give you a full account of our march and fight now as I have no time, but will try if Providence permits to give you a detailed account in a few days if we remain here.

When we arrived here we were all about worn out. I was nearly sick, but a little rest will bring me out all right. I lost ten pounds while on the march. My love to all

Your affect son
Edwin Weller

To Netty Watkins
From Camp of 107th N.Y. VOLs.
Near *Stafford Court House, Va.*
May 13th, 1863

Dear Friend Nett,

Your most welcome and interesting letter of the 8th Inst. was received yesterday and as we are agin under marching orders, and liable to start any day, I concluded it was but for me to answer immediately for if I neglected it a day or two I might not have an opportunity again in some time. I was very glad indeed to hear from you and to hear that you are enjoying yourself *so* well. Life is worth but little unless a person can enjoy it, and my motto is to enjoy life the best way and as much as possible. . . .

Adjt. Hull Fantin has resigned and recvd. an honorable discharge from the service. He started for home yesterday morning. Grove wrote me that his wife had had another sinking spell lately. I fear he will lose Louise. She is a splendid lady and one who would make herself usefull in the world if her health would permit. It seems too bad to have such people taken away just as bright prospects are opening before them of the future. But it is all for the best or it would not be ordered so.

You ask to be forgiven for making such a great mistake as directing a letter Lieut. instead of Sergt. to me. I did not wish you to understand me as finding any fault about it for I supposed that of course you had been informed that I had been promoted or you would not have directed so. I only wish to inform you that such was not the case. I received several letters from other friends about the same time I did yours directed in the same way. So I thought best to correct the mistake, for fear some in the Regt. might think I was getting ahead of my time and wanted to make things appear at Home larger than they really were. It seems that Donnelly circulated, or told among my friends in Havana that I had no doubt received or would receive my commission before he got back to the Regiment, which I had rather he would not have told. This is how all my friends have heard of such a thing. . . .

You say you wish I were there to take dinner with you. You do not wish so any more than I wish I was there. I think I could sit down to a beautifully spread table about now and do great justice to the victuals, but much more would I enjoy the pleasure of your company. Many are the plesant thoughts connected with my association with you Nett, and I look anxiously forward to a time when I will be permitted to see all my friends again and enjoy their society and be assured that you are foremost among them. I often think what a pleasure it would be for me to visit home and friends for a few days but the time that is given on Furloughs now will hardly let a person more than get home and turn around and come back, and another hindrance is that we are just in the midst of the Spring Campaign and I should hate to leave my company or Regt. now. Consequently I consider it best for me to remain till active operations abate and then make a trial.

You have no doubt read the accounts of the recent Battles on the Rappahannock—Our Regt. was all through that fight. We left our camp at Hope Landing on the 26th of April and marched with the rest of our Brigade and Corps, by the way of Kelleys Ford and so to Chancelerville. On Sunday the 2nd Inst. we had a very hard fight with the Rebs. It commenced at daybreak and lasted till nearly noon. Our Brigade was nearly the first in the fight. Our Regiment stood right up to the spot, and done good execution. We

COTTAGE GROVE PUBLIC LIBRARY

were in the fight about 1 1/2 hours fireing steadily and would have stayed longer had our Ammunition not given out and we were relieved by another Brigade.

While in the fight there was a fresh Brigade of Rebs came up and had at their head a Genl. or Colonel, I could not tell which. He was on Horseback and as they came up in mass I showed the boys this officer and told them to let him have it. Immediately about twenty of us levelled our pieces at him and fired and Mr. Gen. or Col. fell, horse and all. Our whole Brigade then pored a terrible volly into them and they were obliged to fall back.

About that time we were relieved by the other Brigade and we left the field. I enjoyed the fireing finely and so did most of the Regt. Our Major was wounded and one Captain killed. The loss in the Regt. was five killed, Fiftyfive wounded and twenty five missing. I came through without a scratch. I hope I may always be as fortunate.

Col. Diven has resigned and gone home. Diven was a brave man but did not know how to command. This is the reason he left I think. The report is that Lt. Col. Crane of the old 23rd is to be our next Col. We hope this is so as he is said to be one of the best military men in the service.

Give my love to Sarah Woodhull, and tell her to be a good girl. Chas. Duryea is still with us and well — he sends regards. I do not think of anything more this time so I will close. Write soon and a good long letter.

Ever Your True Friend
Ed Weller

To Netty Watkins
From Camp of 107th N.Y. Vols.
Near *Stafford C. H., Va.*
June 1st, 1863

Dear Friend Nett,

Your very interesting and welcome letter came to hand a
few days since. I was glad as usual to hear from you. We are
still inactive and doing but little except picket and guard
duty, and drilling occasionally. Since I wrote you before
Capt. Donnelly has resigned and gone home. We regretted
very much his going but had to submit as he was bound to
go. This leaves us without any of our old lot of officers that
came out with us. Lieut. Middleton formally of Co. H. but
now in our Co. is in command.

Charley Duryea has just returned from a visit home and
at Havana on a Furlough of ten days. He reports all well in
Havana, and sayes he had a gay time which I do not doubt.
He was there the evening of the reception of Co. K of the
3rd N.Y.V. and partook of the supper prepared for them.
He said it was a grand affair. He saw your brother Charley.
He brought me several very nice presents from my friends
in Havana.

I had nearly made up my mind to visit home soon as he
returned but the next day after he got back Furloughs were
cut down to Five days, this time. Would not more than give
a person time to get home and come immediately back. So I
have concluded to wait till the time is extended to a longer
time. The reason I think for the time being shortened is on
account of the late movements of the Rebs in the opposite
side of the River. They were expected over this side to make
a dash but I do not think there is any danger now. I

presume we shall get a longer time on Furloughs in August and September.

It seems by what I hear that there was a general rejoicing and celebration North at the news of our occupation of Richmond. It would have been much better if they had waited till the news was fully confirmed. I do not believe in making such demonstrations before there is some certainty of what we are doing.

I have got well recruited from the fatigue of our last march and fight and am now ready for another but I hardly think we shall leave here very soon. Speaking of warm weather, the weather north is not a circumstance to the weather we have here. We have already had as warm weather here as I ever seen or experienced north. The lord only knows what it will be in July, August and September. I do not think the army can move much during these three months. Even now we can not drill between ten A.M. and four P.M.

I do not see but that you are pretty well situated and like your present home well. [Nettie was visiting two married sisters in Union Springs, New York, on Seneca Lake.] I know I should like to live there for a while and take some of those delightful rides. I should enjoy them well. I think the young people very sensible in regard to receiving Beaux on Sunday there. It fully agrees with my views on the subject. I think I shall have to take up my permanent abode in Union Springs when this war is over. I do not see how you can get homesick in so lively a town. I am sure I should not.

I am really sorry for you Nett. You must be lonely. All your lovers gone to war. Surely Havana can not have any attractions for you now. I surmise there is some very nice young man that attracts your attention somewhere in

Cayuga Co. Of course I do not blame you in such a gay town as Union Springs. I presume if I were to go there I should fall in love with some of those nice young damsels. You say you have taken quite a shine to a nice young man there but as bad luck will have it he is engaged as all young men are said to be. Now I will tell you how to bring the thing all O.K. Just go to work and break up the engagement between this young fellow and lady and you are all right.

I fear that you get discouraged to easy Nett. I do not know but I should presume, among the many gentlemen friends that you have, that your matrimonial prospects were pretty good, and should think you are not doomed to remain Nettie Watkins for many years at most, at least I suppose you hope so. Ha, ha. But enough of this nonsense, as you call it. . . .

Since Charly got back I am pretty well posted on Havana matters. I will close. Write soon as convenient for I shall expect an answer in as short a time as it has been since the recpt. of yours.

Your *Affectionate* Friend,
Ed Weller

4

As the war's third summer bloomed, Lee's successes in Northern Virginia freed him for another try at what he had failed to achieve at Antietam—invasion of the North. The Virginia valleys pointing northward were dusty with hordes of gray-clad soldiers all marching in one direction. And the Union forces were wheeling in that direction too, their ranks swelled by new enlistees and conscripts alike, their commanders bent on protecting Washington and making contact with the Rebels before they could inflict fatal damage on the north's fields and cities.

Through June the tension mounted—fearfully in the North, confidently in the South, until finally the fateful contact was made in southern Pennsylvania. There Union and Confederacy faced one another on July first and for three days were locked in awful combat.

The great battle of Gettysburg differed from most others in its spectacular visibility. Even though billowing smoke often obscured parts of the bloody action, the progress could be followed by field glasses and even the naked eye. Flags and shouts and concentrated gunfire all marked the seething movement and in the end, unlike most other battles, the participants knew the winners from the losers. The grisly battlefield itself told the story.

Next day Edwin Weller, as was his custom after battle, wrote his father.

Battlefield Near Gettysburgh Pa
July 5th 1863

Dear Father

I am all safe
have passed through one of the
most fierce and hardest faught
Battles of the war. but thank
fortune the fatal Bullett has
again missed me. We have
been under fire for three days
in succession. our loss I ca
not yet tell what it is.
We drove the Rebs at every point,
and slaughtered them awfully.
We faught the 1st. 2nd & 3rd and
the 4th rested as the Rebs had
withdrew to take a new position
as we supposed. but this morning
the report is that there is nothing
to be found of them in this vacin
ity. We have send a Cavelry and
Infantry force after them. which

will bother them some I think,
We have taken somewhere between
ten and Twenty thousand Prisoners
I learn, I have this morning
been over part of the Battle field
and I never saw a more horrid
sight in my life. Rebels lay on
piles all over the field dead, their
loss is very heavy. they prisoners
admit a very heavy loss.
We are now under marching
orders and and expect to have
a wild Goose Chase after the Rebs
The mail is now ready to leave
and I must close   my love to all
Write Soon   Your affect Son
                    Edwin Weller

News from Gettysburg. *All of Edwin Weller's other letters were written carefully in ink. This one, dated the day after the battle ended, was scribbled more hastily in pencil.*

To Theodore Weller
From *Battlefield Near Gettysburgh, Pa.*
July 5th, 1863

Dear Father,

I am all safe, have passed through one of the most fierce and hardest fought Battles of the war but thank fortune the fatal Bullett has again missed me. We have been under fire for three days in succession, our loss I can not yet tell what it is. We drove the Rebs at every point and slaughtered them awfully. We fought the 1st, 2nd and 3rd, and the 4th rested as the Rebs had withdrew to take a new position as we supposed, but this morning the report is that there is nothing to be found of them in this vacinity. We have send a Cavelery and Infantry force after them which will bother them some I think. We have taken somewhere between ten and twenty thousand prisners I learn. I have this morning been over part of the Battlefield and I never saw a more horrid sight in my life. Rebels lay in piles all over the field dead. Their loss is very heavy. The prisners admitt a very heavy loss. We are now under marching orders and and expect to have a wild goose chase after the Rebs. The mail is now ready to leave and I must close. Write Soon. My love to all

> Your affect Son
> Edwin Weller

To Netty Watkins
From Bivouack of 107th N.Y. Vols.
Near *Fairplay, Md.*
July 12, 1863

Dear Friend Nett,

Your long looked for and much welcomed letter of the 21st ultimo was received about a week ago. You are no doubt aware of some of the movements of the Army of the Potomac. We left Stafford C.H., Va. on the 13th of June and have been on the continual go ever since.

We had the pleasure of participating in the three days fight at Gettysburgh if it can be called a pleasure. We succeeded in giving the Rebs a good sound thrasing, one which they will long remember I think. It was a horrible sight to pass over the Battlefield the next day after the Fight and see the dead Rebs. literally piled up all along our line of battle. Also the houses in the vacinity either burned or pierced through and through with shell or solid shot. I cannot give you any idea of the appearance of the Battlefield after a fight. A person to get an idea of the devastation etc. must visit one.

The fourth day we discovered that the Rebs had skedaddled bag and baggage but had left their dead and most of their wounded in our hands. We of course buried their dead and took care of their wounded, over six hundred of which were looked after in our Corps Hospital.

OVERLEAF   After the Battle. *On the same day Edwin Weller wrote to his father from Gettysburg, this photo of Union dead was made by Timothy O'Sullivan, one of several commercial photographers who hastily trundled up in their wagon darkrooms to record the grim scene.*

Our cavellry were immediately sent in persuit of the enemy to learn the direction they had taken and harrass them as much as possible. Consequently you see that I spent the fourth in rather a quiet manner for me—rested most of the day.

It rained nearly all day the fourth at Gettysburgh. On the morning of the 5th we received marching orders and started in persuit of the enemy but did not come up to them till we reached Crampton Gap in the Blue Ridge mountains. Since then we have had several skirmishes with the Rebs and have kept driving them back till we have got them into what we call a tight place and no way for them to get across the river if they want to.

Our Regt. and the 3rd Wis. came out to our present position on a reconnaisance last eve. about ten o'clock. Took position in a cornfield where the mud was about three inches deep, it having rained for two days previous and were obliged to lay down and I must say I enjoyed my nights rest finely. My bed consisted of young corn that I pulled up and lay down.

This morning the rest of our Brigade came up to us which consists of three Regiments more. Our skirmishers are now out about one half mile from us, pecking away at the Rebs as fast as they show themselves.

As I sit here writing in the shade of a large Oak tree, I can hear heavy cannonading and musketry on the right of us about five miles. I judge it is on our extreme right. We are expecting any moment to be called upon to try our hand at the Rebs and I hope we shall when called on, give them a good whipping.

I am glad you are having such fine times at the Springs. I almost envy you your enjoyment, at least I should very much like to participate in Some of those gay times you are having but I shall have to be content till I can once more be free. I received a letter from Grove a few days since. He gave me a discription of his visit to the Falls. I judge he had a gay time by his tell. You ask me if I ever met a certain Leuit. since I have been out. I do not recollect of ever meeting one by that name. I have been introduced to a good many different Leuitenants and men of the army but do not recollect but very few of their names. It may be that I met such a gentleman but I can not now bring him to mind.

I really wish I might have been at Union Springs the evening you speak of. It would afforded me a great deal of pleasure to have administered the said arm poltice. You know there is nothing that pleases me more than a job of that kind. It has been so long since I administered on of that kind of poltice that it might come rather unhandy, but I think I would make a trial of there was a chance. But I must close as I have a letter to write home yet today and we are expecting to move soon. Remember me to Sarah Woodhull. Excuse haste, and write soon as possible.

From your Friend
Ed Weller

5

After Gettysburg, the war entered a new phase, and so did the fortunes of the 107th New York Volunteers and Edwin Weller.

For the 107th the big change was shifting from the Eastern Theater of Operations to the West, where Grant's Vicksburg victory was reshaping the military picture.

Now the 107th became part of the Army of the Cumberland in south-central Tennessee, a few miles north of the Alabama state line, deep inside the shrinking South. After a year of fighting in Virginia, in Maryland and in Pennsylvania, most of it defensive in character, the new scene was the Secesh heartland and the Union soldiers were on the offensive.

For most of the New Yorkers it was their first glimpse of the Deep South. Here they came into much closer contact with civilians. The New Yorkers became Occupiers as well as active combatants, and between Occupiers and Occupied all kinds of strange attractions and revulsions seem bound to happen, as Americans in later generations were to learn vividly.

Edwin Weller's letters reflect many facets of these shifting relationships, but even more they reflect a new warmth in his relationship with Nettie. The reason seems to be that between Gettysburg and Tennessee he had been home for a long stay and had seen a good deal of her.

In mid-July Edwin had been detailed back to Elmira and Havana on a recruiting mission along with others from every company in the regiment. Combat, disease, and desertion had thinned the 107th ranks and recruits were needed. And for him it was no doubt the most welcome of assignments.

Nettie, the youngest of a large family, was living with her sister and brother-in-law, Louisa and Daniel Tracy, in Havana, where Edwin had clerked in Tracy's dry-goods store. The Tracys had two small children, and Nettie seems to have served often as a convenient babysitter while she was being courted.

But it couldn't last forever, and by the beginning of December he was back on field duty, writing letters.

To Nettie Watkins
From Detachment 107th N.Y.V.
Near *Wartrace, Tenn.*
Monday, Dec. 14th, 1863

Dear Friend Nett,

I was last Saturday the happy recipient of your letter dated the 7th Inst. and this afternoon finds me seated at my wide table in my office attempting to scribble you a few lines in return. I presume you have received a letter from me, ere this, of the 3rd Inst. written immediately after my arrival here. I was glad to hear that you were well, and everything progressing about the same as when I left.

You speak of it seeming lonely to you after I left, I had hardly thought that my presence among you had been of *particular* interest to any *one* of my lady friends but I am nevertheless very happy to know that someone looks back to my association with them with pleasure. For a while after I got here it seemed odd to me, that I could not drop down to Havana every few days and have a nice sociable time with some of my friends. It will no doubt be many days before I shall have that privilage again but do not for a moment think or say that I may never return to see my friends of H. again. I know such a thing is possible but I never allow myself to think of such a thing.

I am like you, only look on the brightest side of the picture. I have always thought and calculated that I should live to get back and enjoy citizen life again, and hope such may be my luck.

You asked me if I ever think of our ride over to Trumansburgh. Indeed I do, and with much pleasure too, notwithstanding the hard rain, and poor rig we had to endure. But allow me to warn you to be careful about leaving your Hdkf. and Hairpins in the bottom of carriages or sleighs this winter for they might be found and forwarded to you as they once was. Nett you would be surprised to see me up to Havana again this winter, would you not? Such a thing is not impossible. Our regiment is talking very strongly of reinlisting to serve for three years from the first of January and if it does, the whole Regt. will go to Elmira to recruit up to the maximum number. We shall know in a few days what will be done in reference to it. If we go we shall start sometime in January and remain there about three months. . . .

Just three weeks ago last night I was enjoying myself so well in your company at D. Tracys. Well you may speak of that as a pleasant time and in fact the whole three last nights of my stay in Havana were spent very pleasantly by me. Never have I been in your society Nett, but that I have had a pleasant time and I sincerely hope that I may when this cruel War is over, return among friends whose society I have enjoyed so well.

I am expecting to have a new lot of photographs in a week or so and think they will be better than the one I sent you. If they are, I will exchange with you. Will Byron has been here to see me. He came on last Saturday afternoon and stayed at Bridgeport. He has been in the hospital there for about six weeks, has got well enough to travel about, so came up to see me. He is looking quite well now but I can see that he has been quite sick. We had a gay time talking over the old times we had when in Havana. He told me some things that I never dreamed of before. . . .

Do you ever hear from Sarah Woodhull. When you write her remember me to her. The weather has been very warm here since I returned, until today which is quite cold. I am expecting to go to Tallahema tomorrow or next day to get mustered as Leuitenant, in order to draw Leuitenants pay. Well I must close as I have got some new clothing to issue to the Brigs. and it must be done before dark. Remember me to Mr. and Mrs. Tracy. Tell Miner to not do too heavy picket duty and when he does to try and get relieved at the proper times. Also tell him when on picket to look out for *Dorgs* that growl. Also remember me to Call. Write soon and believe me ever your Friend,

Ed Weller

To Netty Watkins
From — Detachment 107th N.Y.V.
Near *Wartrace, Tenn.*
Thursday, *Dec. 24th, 1863*

Dear Friend Nett,
    Your very welcome and highly interesting letter of the
13th Inst. was duly received last Sunday and my duties not
being very arduous today, I thought I could not better
improve my time than by replying to your kind letter. I am
glad you are so punctual in answering my letter, also that
you appreciate them so well, for I certainly am always very
glad to receive and read and reread your good letters.
    I am enjoying the best of health at present and hope you
are equally well blessed. You are very right in believing a
letter from friends always acceptably received by a soldier.
It is indeed a great pleasure to think that friends whom we
highly esteem think of us occasionally, especially those far
away. I have often thought to myself, what would we poor
mortals do if we could not write our thoughs and desires on
paper and have them conveyed to friends. It would indeed
be a sad state of affairs, but thank fortune such is not the
case.
    I am happy to hear that I am wrong in supposing that my
friendship for you might be without a return. But on the
other hand that you value my friendship as highly as I possibly can yours. You say a great deal and possibly more
than you imagin you are when you say *that*, for believe me
when I say that since I first became acquainted with you I
have esteemed you *very highly*. And when, away down here
in Tennessee, I recall the many happy hours I have spent in
your society, I wonder if I shall ever have the pleasure of
enjoying that society again as I have in days past. I sincerely

COTTAGE GROVE PUBLIC LIBRARY

hope such may be my lot for it will certainly be a happy one.

I am glad to hear that you still have occasionally a social party in your quiet village. You no doubt had very social times at Mrs. McGuires and Octaves. I should think Octaves would be a good place to go for fun. I should think the young men of Havana would make a move toward getting up some kind of fun the winter. I think I should make a move in that direction if I were there. But it seems that all the young men who used to be foremost in such matters have steadyed down, and have had their attention drawn off to an object of some kind that occupies all their time.

Havana seemed much different in some respects when I was there from what it did before I entered the Army. I expect when I return from the Army (if I ever should be so fortunate) that I shall find many of my old comrads and associates of both sex married and gone, at least things look very favorable in that direction now I think. . . .

I am sorry on you girls and boys accounts that you are not to have church anymore Sabbath evenings. What is the cause of breaking up these evening meetings? It really is too bad. I should like to have been there to attend Mr. Chesters donation last week, but it is otherwise ordered, my country requires my services here. My country first and pleasure when my services is no longer wanted here, is my motto.

I am now in command of our company, the Captain having gone away on a military visit for two or three days. Yesterday my company was inspected by an inspecting officer and gave me the credit of having the best looking Company and camp on this line of R.R. defences.

The weather here is quite cold today for this southern country but still is nowhere near as cold as the weather north. I see by your letter you are having pretty cold weather north now. I am sorry that you are suffering so with the cold nights. It would afford me pleasure to administer to your wants as far as keeping you warm in my old style if I were only there, but as such is not the case you must take my good will for the deed. And you see Nett, that I have not forgot any old failings. I should think you would learn to skate. It is a very fine exercise and nice sport. I would not mind taking a good skate today with you if I were up there.

There is to be a Christmas Party about two miles from here at a place called Bell Buckle tomorrow night. I have an invitation to attend but hardly know whether I shall go or not. There is a few very good looking ladies up there, and will be at the party I am told. I shall have a gay old time if I do go you can bet.

I have visits from ladies every day, to obtain passes to go to some of the villages along our lines. Most of the young ladies here ride on horseback and they are as a general thing very fine riders too. Charley Duryea is visiting a young lady not far from camp occasionally. She is quite a gay female. I have not made a very extensive acquaintance here yet, must rush around a little I guess and find what is in this part of Tennessee. No more this time. Remember me to all my Friends. Write soon, I am as Ever your Affectionate Friend

E. Weller

P.S. I wish you a Merry Christmas and happy New Year. Hope you may enjoy them as well as we did two years ago.

Ed.

To Netty Watkins
From Headquarters Detachment 107th N.Y.V.
Near *Wartrace, Tenn.*
Jany 22, 1864

Dear Friend Nett,

After nearly two weeks of anxious waiting I yesterday had the pleasure of once more perusing another of your interesting letters. I had almost come to the conclusion that you had forgotten that there was such a fellow as Ed Weller in the Army suffering and bleeding for his country, but not so yet.

I was down to the village of Wartrace when your letter arrived and did not get back till late last night. I had the pleasure while there of seeing a wedding party arrive there, the first I have seen since I arrived here. It was that of a soldier of the 46th Pennsylvania Regt. He married a young lady living a short distance from Wartrace.

I should judge by the appearance and looks of the lady that she did not amount to any considerable sum. The sister of the lady and another soldier accompanied them on their tour. The appearance of both was particularly striking. They wore light calico or homespun dresses which came down within about a foot of the ground. Then their hats or jockeys were of the style worn north about four years ago with the rim turned down all around. The rest of their wearing apparel I will not attempt to describe for language here fails to be adequate for a proper discription. But take them all in all they were a decidedly gay couple.

I was out calling last week among the fair damsels of Tennessee. We have a Glee Club in our Co. and one night last week they invited me to go out with them to call on some ladies living a short distance from the camp. Of course

I could not refuse, so went. We found four very fair looking young ladies there and passed the evening with them very pleasantly. The boys sang for them after which by prevailing pretty hard we got the ladies to sing the celebrated southern song, The Bonny Blue Flag. It is a very pretty thing, but the sentiments are wrong. After hearing that we left with a strong invitation to call soon again. I am going to call on two young ladies tomorrow who live about three miles above here. They have a piano and are said to be good players and singers beside being good looking. I anticipate a gay time.

There is a detail of officers and men about starting from our Regt. for York state to recruit for our Regt. Our Capt. is to go with the detail which will leave me in command of the company while he is absent.

I expect then my time will be more fully occupied than it is now. Our Regt. have given up reinlisting for three years longer for very good reasons. viz — that no troops who have not been in the field over two years are not allowed to reinlist. Our time is now a little over half out. The time will soon fly away here in the army. . . .

I have had come new photographs sent me which I think much better than the others and I will send you one if you like it better than the other one I sent you a short time ago you may keep it and send me the other in your next letter. I had these last ones taken for the officers of our Regt. who have wanted my photograph ever since I returned but I thought I would let some of my friends have the best of exchanging and giving some of the officers those I had taken first.

How well I should like to drop in and see your occasionly and allay some of your lonely hours. Nothing would give me more pleasure. Well, I must close. Write as

soon and often as you can Nett, and I will do the same.
Remember me to Mr. and Mrs. Tracy and family, also to all
the young people who may enquire after me. Believe me
ever your sincere Friend,

Ed

To Nettie Watkins
From Camp of Detachment 107 N.Y.V.
Near *Wartrace, Tenn.*
Feby 10th, 1864

Dear Friend Nett,

Your letter was received two or three days since and you
shall be gratified with a reply at this, my earliest opportunity. I am always very glad to hear from you, and what I like
best is early replies to my letters. I always make it a point to
answer all letters I receive at the earliest possible time. And
believe me when I say that there is no one, from whom I receive letters, that I took more anxiously for letters from than
I do you.

I jumped on the train this morning and went to the
Village of Wartrace — have just returned. This is the Second
time I have sat down and wrote you a letter after being at
Wartrace. It has only happened so however.

I saw two very fine looking young ladies there who were
in a store trading. Of course I wanted to get a peep at the
gay damsels, so stepped in the store pretending I wanted to
buy something and inquired for an article that I knew they
did not have. I got a good glimpse of them and found out
before I left who they were and where they lived.

You are pretty near right in thinking that we soldiers like the ladies as well as they do us. If we did not we would be singular beings I think. If the ladies think as much of us as we do of them they think considerable of us.

So for there being more "hearts than lives lost" here, during our stay in the South, I can not say. I have no doubt but there will be some hearts lost but I imagin the loss will be mostly among the ladies, for the soldiers as a general thing do not think them quite equal to the "Girls they left behind them," and all I have got to say to them is, if any of them are foolish enough to fall in love with me, they must pick themselves up again.

I fear if we all should follow the example of that soldier of the 46th and return with each a Southern Bell on his arm, there would be many wounded hearts among the northern ladies. And of course we do not wish to cause any more misery than there is now among the fair sex. And then it would be injuring the cause too much in the north — you perceive, don't you? that I am looking to you northern ladies interest, it is so.

I was very much surprised to hear that Miss Fellows should be so much interested in me as to wish my photograph but if she can see anything about my ugly Phiz that is interesting she is welcome to it but I think it would be no more than fair and just that she should return the compliment by sending me her Carte-de-Visite. Please give her my kindest regards.

I am very glad to hear that you young folks of H. are enjoying yourselves so well this winter with parties. Skating etc. Wish I might be there a few days to enjoy some of the fine skating you are having there. I was always a great lover of skating although not much of a skater. . . .

Then you need some recruits in the line of young men in

Havana do you? I rather think the chances are that before a very long time, you will need more than you now do, for it is very evident that there will many of them have to enlist soon or be drafted for the President has called for half a million more troops. I gladly join with you in hoping that day not far distant when this Cruel War shall end, and I may once more, if but for a short time, enjoy the society of my friends in Havana. I flatter myself that I have some good friends there.

What a girl you are Nett. Always imagining that you are getting so much nonsense in your letters. Now I want you to write everything you can think of when you write me just as though you had been acquainted with me all your life, and write me good long letters. If I do not complain I am sure you had not ought to. I am getting so that I can not write a letter any more on one sheet — can not condense my ideas enough. I have no doubt but that I get a great deal superfluous matter in my letters but it is just as I think when I am writing.

I have just had to stop writing to entertain a couple of ladies who came here to get a pass. They were very sociable. One was a married lady and the other was a young lady and a relative of the married lady. I was joking with them about hardtack. I told her it was a bargan and I would give her all the hardtack she wanted in exchange. The young lady said she liked my quarters pretty well but thought she would not stay. So I did not make such a bargan after all.

I have many calls from ladies here, for passes. I had a call from a northern lady a few days ago, a Lieuts. wife of our Regt. whom is here visiting him. I am now all alone here in my glory, being the only commissioned officer left here with the Co. Our Capt. has gone north on recruiting Service and the 2nd Lieut, is on duty at Wartrace. So that leaves me in command of the Co. Detachment and post.

I am expecting Brig Genl. Rogers commanding our Brigade here tomorrow to make me a call and look at the condition of my post and company. Our Co. was inspected a few days ago and reported by the inspecting officer the best Co. in the Brigade. Well I must stop or I shall fill every space on this sheet. Remember me to all my friends and write me soon for your letters are always thankfully received and read with the most of pleasure. Hoping to hear from you soon I am ever

Your true Friend
Ed Weller

P.S. I was wishing while writing this letter that I should love to be where Charley Duryea imagined me, when writing me while I was home, tonight on a sofa with my arms full of calico or any other kind of goods, only that it contained a nice young lady. Say one about your size and I think should surely have a go-away-trouble expression on my face, if such was the case. I do not know whether you would enjoy it or not — but think you would. I would risk it if I were that woman.

Ed.

Fragment
Likely from Wartrace, Tenn.
Between mid-February and mid-March 1864

I took a trip to the celebrated village of Shelbyville that
we read so much about in *"Uncle-Toms Cabin,"* last week. A
part of our Regt. is stationed there and I went on a sort of
visiting excursion. The night I arrived there the officers had
a dance, but on account of its raining there was not a very
large attendance. I should think about twelve or fifteen
couples. But it went off very nice. The "elite" of the town
were there. There was some very fine looking young ladies
there. The dance broke up about three o'clock.

The next day I called, in company with a Lieut. Shep-
perd, on some young ladies in the aristocratic part of the
town. They were Secesh but very fine looking ladies, the
best I have seen in my travels in the south. We had a very
fine time, got pretty well acquainted with three or four of
(what they call here), the aristocracy of the south. They
gave me a very polite invitation to call on them if I ever
come in Shelbyville again. I think I shall accept this kind invitation if I should ever go there again.

I think you must have had a decidedly gay party at your
house the night they stayed till two o'clock. I am considerable surprised that you should entertain company so late,
knowing your custom to be entirely to the contrary when I
was home, especially the night we was on picket down to
Calls.

The most audacious thing I have heard of in a long time
is the blowing out of the light that night. If I had been there
I should have found out who the person was that dared to
commit such a depredation and no doubt have had him
court marshalled and probably shot. For it is a very grave

act. Of course if I had been there I should not have stayed so late and then when the light was blown out I should got out of the house as soon as possible, if I had been obliged to go out the back door and over the garden fence to get away from the house. You know me well enough to believe all I say, of course you do.

I should like to be there to your fair very much. I hope you may all have a grand time, and the fair be a success for the cause for which it is gotten up is certainly a good one. . . .

I see you do not have much confidence in the stead-fastness of the young ladies as a class. Well it is hard to tell where to find them. They are a fickle race I know, but I always make due allowances for their fickleness, knowing them to be the weakest sex. Of course you are not fickle, Nett. It is not your disposition. I am of the opinion that you are 'installed Chief boss' of the house at D.T.'s, very often are you not? I think by the time you and Mr. Vail hitch your fortunes together you will be pretty well posted in all the departments of housekeeping etc.

You seem to think there is more danger of my falling in love with the ladies here, than there is in the ladies falling in love with me. That may be the case, but I can't see it. I have made up my mind to wait till this cruel war is over and then if I take the foolish notion of marrying into my head, I shall select me a nice sensible northern young lady for my victim or my better half. What do you think of my plan? Is it a safe one?

Tell Miss Fellows I shall expect her photograph as soon as she gets them. Charley Duryea sends regards. Well I must close. I fear you will have a hard stint to read this scribbling. Two sheets full again, what a fellow I am to stretch out a yarn. Remember me to Mr. and Mrs. Tracy

and all my friends. Write me soon. Your letters are so interesting that I like to hear from you often.

Your sincere friend
Ed.

To Netty Watkins
From Camp Detachment 107th N.Y. Vols.
Near *Wartrace, Tenn.*
March 21st, 1864

Dear Friend Nett,

Your very interesting letter of the 13th Inst. came to hand
yesterday (Sunday) and was perused with the greatest of
pleasure. Allow me to repeat, what I have said before that
there is no one of my correspondents whose letters are
hailed with the pleasure yours are. I always find in them
news and sentiments which no others possess — not withstanding the idea you have of your letters containing so
much nonsense. . . .

I am glad to hear that your Fair was such a splendid success. It shows that the people of Havana are yet wide awake
and take an interest in the comforts of the soldiers and the
amount realized will no doubt do much toward relieving
the poor wounded and suffering soldier in the field. I have
no doubt that many times the luxuries, clothing etc. furnished by the sanitary commission, does more toward the
relief of the sick and wounded soldiers than all the surgeons
do. No one can know how much good is done by the Sanitary Commission who is not in the Army. . . .

I should think it would have seemed strange to have the
old people that have always been opposed to dancing

present and get up the supper. I begin to think that H. is under going quite a change in some respects. It is not likely that they would have taken the pains they did, had it not been for benefit of the Fair.

Why did you not tell me the whole of your fortune which was told you. No doubt the news that you were eventually to be married was gratifying, but I hardly think I should like to be told that I was to endure a long sickness before-hand, but if she only made out a good fortune in all other respects, it is not so bad.

I have not had the said Lieuts wives since I wrote you last but am expecting them here today. They may not come as it is rather unplesant today. You wonder they dare trust their wives with me—the reason is, that they know I am perfectly safe, and their ladies (or any other woman) is safe with me.

Then you do think that it is the duty of every young man to marry. Well it is owning to circumstances whether it is their duty or not. If a young man has the wherewith to support a wife as he should, or is in a business that he is sure will furnish the means, then I think he is justified in marrying. But this idea of marrying and not know where tomorrows subsistence is coming from is rather a hard way of living in my opinion.

I should really like to know what John Jessop wanted of a wife just as he is about leaving for the army. There will be widows enough in the country who were married before the war broke out (and their husbands in the Army) without men just going out to get married and then what can he leave for the support of a wife. I fear she will see some pretty tough times unless she has got parents that are able to look to her wants.

You may think I am getting off quite a sermon on matrimony so I will close up the subject by saying that I am an ardent admirer of the institution but my views of the institution differ somewhat from most other mens. Your opinion of my future plans is highly satisfactory, I see you agree with me on some points at least. I suppose you give the cases of Jessop and Miner B. to show the fickleness of men. I do not call it fickleness but a plan they have resorted to to carry out certain ends, which I will not mention. You must not judge the whole of mankind by the trickery of two of the sex. . . .

Then Mr. Vail is really going to marry and settle down in H. is he? Who is to be the happy sharer of his fortune? Anyone in Havana?

Our singing school has closed; we had some gay scenes while it lasted. There is to be preaching in a church about a mile from camp next Sunday. I intend to go if the Rebs do not drive us out of our camp before that time. I have received a dispatch nearly every night for a week past to be on the alert for the Rebs. There is a force of guerrillas prowling up and down the country near the R.R. trying to get below us to the road to destroy the track. They made a dash to the road about twenty miles from us, and attacked a train, ran it off the track and burned it, killing three niggers and taking seven soldiers prisioners. They paroled them after robing them of their jewelry, money and clothes. Our soldiers killed a few of the gang.

Last Thursday night about eleven o'clock two bush-wackers attacked one of my picket posts and attempted to shoot the sentinel but he saw them and commanded them to halt then they shot and ran but did not hit their mark. The sentinel returned the fire and then gave the alarm. I was just getting to sleep but I heard the report of the guns and was out in less than five minutes, got the Co. up ready for an emergency and established a line of pickets around and out a short distance from camp so that they could not surprise us from any direction if there was much of a force of them. But by sending out a squad of men as skirmishers I found that they had all skedaddled.

The Colonel came up to find out the cause of the fireing the next morning and after giving an account of it, he gave me orders to go out to all the houses of citizens within two miles and search all houses for firearms, who did not have a permit from the military commander to keep them.

I only found one man who had no papers and he was a malicious looking fellow. He declared he had no arms about his house but I did not propose to take his word and told him I should be obliged to search his house. He saw I was bound to do it and finally said he had a pistol and Bowing knife. He produced them and I found instead of having a pistol, he had a large revolver such as is carried by our cavelery. I took possession of that and then commenced search and after a thorough examination of the house, I found concealed in the different beds between the ticks one government rifle, loaded, one sword, one cartridge and cap box all of which I took possession of and handed over to the Colonel.

You would have been pleased if you could have seen me hauling their beds etc. hunting after the arms. There was two very fair looking ladies visiting there, who witnessed the proceedings. They hardly knew what to make of it — judging by their appearance. I should have arrested the man had he not produced the Amnesty oath which he had taken a few days before.

Well I must bring my letter to a close for I have already written much more than I expected to when I commenced, as you will see, for I had to come from the second sheet again before I could finish my story. But Nett, I love to write to *you* and when I get started it is hard to bring a letter to a close. You wrote me such a good letter that I fear you will find this a poor return of the compliment.

Our Co. Glee club is now in my quarters singing. They sing splendidly. I am still all alone in the command of this Detachment, and am kept pretty close to camp. Kind regards to Mr. and Mrs. Tracy also Sarah Woodhull and all others who may inquire after me. Write soon. My best wishes to your dear self and for welfare ever

From Your Friend
Ed Weller

From Camp Detachment 107th N.Y.V.
Near *Wartrace, Tenn.*
April 14th, 1864

Dear Friend Nett,

On the 11th Inst. I was again the happy reciepient of an-other of your good and interesting letters. The next day after I recvd. your letter I was summoned to Tallahoma, the HeadQuarters of our Corps, to attend court martial. I was there two days. We tried one case of an attempt at murder and several other smaller ones. I returned last evening. You must not think it strange if this letter is dry and dull, as I am not feeling much like writing letters today. I have not slept much for the last three nights, and have been so situated that it was impossible for me to sleep during the days. I have just been out and played a few games of ball to wake myself up a little. . . .

When I wrote you last I expected we would move before this time, but we are yet in our old location and no signs of our immediate movement toward the front. The 11th and 12th Army corps have lately been consolidated into one, to be called the 1st Corps and to be commanded by the gallant General Joe Hooker. We regret very much indeed to lose our former commander of the 12th corps, Gen'l Slocum, as he was a splendid officer and a gentleman in every respect. But we are fully satisfied that Gen'l Hooker will maintain our former reputation in the new corps.

There is no news here at present of much importance. One of my picket posts was attacked a few nights ago but those who attacked the sentinel did not have very good success. When they attempted to fire on the sentinel their guns did not go off, nothing but the caps cracked. The sentinel saw them as soon as their guns failed to go and fired into them, but did not suppose he hit either of them. But today I have heard that a man suspected of that kind of business died very suddenly yesterday and some of the citizens report that he was shot some way and I presume it is the same fellow. Well if he is the fellow he has got his just deserts.

I see that Molly's rooms are quite a resort yet for the young folks to go and have a gay and festive time occasionally. Indeed, what gay stories those rooms of hers would tell if they could talk. I should hardly like to be present at the rehearsal of them for fear that I might come in for a share in many. Then Doc Wells and Priss Tillotson have really hitched fortunes? Good for them. I wish them all the happiness and luck imaginable. . . .

I do not see as this War makes a very great difference in young folks getting married. They are all bound to marry I believe. What queer notions some people will get into their heads. Two weddings has occured in Havana within a short time. Who comes next? I am expecting to hear before many months of some of you young ladies (my old associates in society) emigrating to the state of matrimony and settle down for life. We poor soldier boys will have to make an entire new start when we go home, I expect. . . .

The Lieutenants and wives whom I mentioned as visiting me some time ago were up and made me another visit a few days ago. Had a gay time as usual. You still remember those very plesant and happy evenings we spent together while I was at home, I see. Yes and so does your humble servant E.W. I shall always remember them with much interest and many is the time I have thought of these visits and other plesant times enjoyed with my dear friend Miss N.L.W. and may kind providence permit me again when this cruel strife is over to meet dear friends and enjoy many more happy hours in their society. Well I will close, as what few ideas I had have all been taken out of my noodle. Hoping to hear from you soon. I am truely your friend and well wisher.

Edwin Weller

Direct as before at present.

P.S. Encluded I send you a Holly leaf. These are Green the year round and look very nice in winter.

Ed.

6

Catching bushwhackers, guarding railroads, giving out civilian passes, these were all quiet, amiable duties busying the 107th that winter in Tennessee, and Edwin Weller's letters give no hint he was aware, as he must have been, of decisive battles being fought not far away. Chickamauga, Lookout Mountain, Missionary Ridge — these are great names in the Civil War battle roster and all had been fought in the closing weeks of 1863, until finally Tennessee was cleared of major Rebel forces and the Union forces stood poised to menace Georgia.

President Lincoln, happy at last to have a winning general, summoned General Grant back east to command the Army of the Potomac while making Major General William T. Sherman commander of the West.

Their grand strategy was clear — for Sherman to plunge into Georgia, take Atlanta, sweep on to the sea and then turn north to link up with Grant. That of course is what happened, but it took a long, toilsome, bitter year of warfare to accomplish and leave the South shattered in defeat.

The names of Sherman's Georgia battles are not as instantly recognizable as Gettysburg or Antietam or The Wilderness, but they are nonetheless crucial; these are the engagements through which Edwin Weller and the 107th regiment passed as spring turned into summer — the battles of Resaca and of Dallas Gap, the siege of Atlanta.

The 107th saw far more continuous front-line combat than in earlier years. Edwin Weller's role as a commissioned officer —only a lieutenant to be sure—gave him greater responsibilities and a new, youthful gravity. He talks more frequently of the chances of survival. He shows compassion for war victims. He begins to define his plans for a post-war life, "if nothing happens to me." And most importantly for Nettie, he slowly reaches a great decision. It is halting and low-keyed in statement, but deeply passionate.

From Bivouack of 107th N.Y.V.
Snake Creek Cap— 15 miles in rear Dalton, Ga.
May 12th 1864

Dear Friend Nettie,
Your very welcome and interesting letter of the 2nd Inst. was received a few days since. I was more glad than ever to hear from you, being so far from direct communication with the North. Letters from those I deem dear friends seem doubly dear to receive letters from at this time of expected conflict with the enemy. This letter will not reach you till after the present campaign is over, there being an order against sending letters any farther than Nashville until this movement is over. But I thought I would write you as this would probably reach you three or four days before one would if written after the campaign is over.
We broke camp near Wartrace the 27th of April and arrived here day before yesterday having marched about one

hundred and fifty miles. Passed through Bridgeport Ala, Chattanooga Tenn. and Ringgold Ga. We are now in possession of this Gap and holding it so the Rebs if they retreat can not get through this way. The canons are now booming away on the left of our line of battle, near Dalton, fifteen miles distant. How soon we may be engaged we know not, we are awaiting orders to move forward. We are at present five miles from our main line of Battle. I hope I shall have the luck I have had in former battles to get through safe and without harm.

I see that my friends, or whatever they may be, must have got about out of material to gossip about as they have taken up my name for a subject. Still I do not think I feel very bad over it. There is one consolation, while they are talking about us they are talking about no one else. I am sure, I might feel myself a lucky fellow if such was the case, for there is certainly no one of my young lady acquaintances whom I have a higher regard or esteem for than I do your own fair self. The same has been said in regard to us before you know. I can not imagin however, who could have been the person so well acquainted with my affairs as to know much more about them than myself. I presume the next letter I receive from Leroy he will have something to say in regard to the matter. But whoever it was conjectured much much more than they know to be true.

I do really wish I might be with you to help you keep house while Daniels folks are in N.Y. for I know I could enjoy myself hugely. Hope I may ere many months have the privilage of meeting you and enjoying your social society. Now Nett, I never want you to say another word about your letters seeming to you so uninteresting. When I complain then it is time for you to say something about your letters being uninteresting. . . .

COTTAGE GROVE PUBLIC LIBRARY

Well, I shall be obliged to close as the mail will leave in a few moments. I will write you again after the Battle if nothing happens to me. Write soon as you get this. Love to Leroy. Kind regards to D. Tracy and family. Love to your own dear self.

Your friend,
Ed Weller

Direct your letter hereafter to

Lt. E. Weller
Co. H. — 107th N.Y. Vols.
1st Division, 20th Corps
Army Cumberland via Nashville, Tenn.

From Bivouack of 107th N.Y. Vols.
Cassville, Ga.
May 22nd, 1864

Dear Friend Nettie,
    I wrote you nearly two weeks ago — immediately after the reciept of your letter and before the battle of Resaca. Since that time we have passed through a pretty hard fight but I was fortunate and came through untouched by the bullet. We defeated the Rebs and compelled them to fall back some forty miles. They are now some fourteen miles distant from here on the Blue Ridge and I suppose fortifying themselves.

The Road to Atlanta

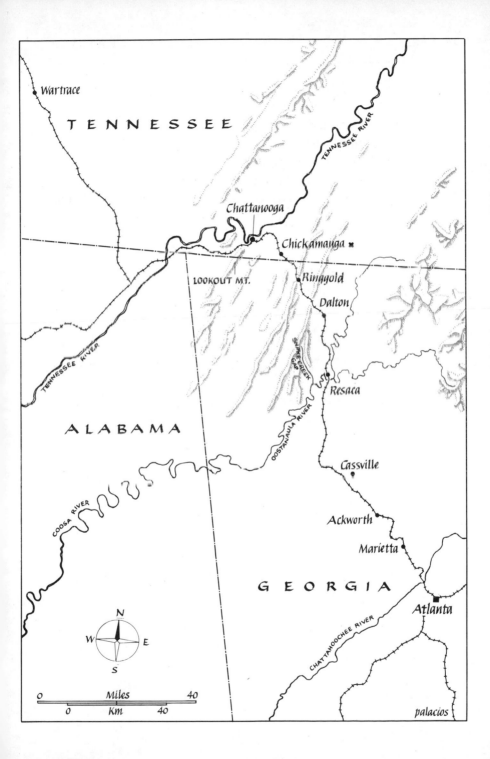

Wartrace

T E N N E S S E E

TENNESSEE RIVER

Chattanooga

Chickamauga ✷

LOOKOUT MT.

Ringgold

Dalton

TENNESSEE RIVER

SNAKE CREEK GAP

OOSTANAULA RIVER

Resaca

A L A B A M A

Cassville

COOSA RIVER

Ackworth

Marietta

G E O R G I A

Atlanta

N
W   E
S

CHATTAHOOCHEE RIVER

0   Miles   40

0   Km   40

palacios

We have been here three days now resting out and getting ready for another forward movement. We are to start tomorrow again after the Rebs and I presume will see some hard fighting before this campaign is over.

The loss in our Regt. during the late fight was slight — two killed and seven wounded. Among the wounded was our Leiut. Colonel (Fox). We only had one man wounded in our company. The 141st N.Y. is now in our Division and were engaged in the fight. Their loss is quite heavy. Eleven killed and over seventy wounded. Only one of the Havana boys was wounded and that was Jack McDonald — His wound is said to be very dangerous. All the other boys from Havana in the Regt. are well. I was over to their Regt. last night and saw most of the boys.

Bryon, Charley Durkee and Charley Curgell are well, and looking fine. They are all the same old boys. I do not see as Durkee has changed in the least. I will not give you a discription of the battle as I have written to Leroy today and given him an account of it and if you would like to see it, read his letter.

We officers have been obliged to send all our baggage to the rear — and come down to the same rations that the Privates live on. Can not get anything else unless we forage for it. I have a man out when on the march foraging for fresh meat — chickens, garden sauce etc. So I think I shall make out to live. I can live on the same rations that the privates do. I have done it once and can do the same again. A soldier can accustom himself to anything if he is obliged to. Such is the case with me. . . .

This state is one of the finest I have ever been in south. The country is beautiful. Flower gardens numerous and all in bloom. I have had several very fine bouquets during my stay here. I have often wished when in possession of a nice bouquet that I might have the pleasure of presenting you with a rich bouquet. It would no doubt be a great rarity to you. I have also had a mess of green peas since I came here.

I shall send this letter by a Mass. soldier who leaves for home today. It is said that our mail does not go any farther than Nashville till this campaign is over but I can not vouch for the truth of the rumer. So I have taken this course to get a letter through to you. Well, I must close as one of the men is waiting to take this to the man who is to carry it. Write as soon as you can for I am anxious to hear from you. Kind regards to Daniel and wife and all others who may inquire after me. . . .

Now Nett I want you to write me as often as you can and I shall do the same. All my letters may not get through till after this campaign is over but all letters coming from the North will come through to the Army. Regards to Miss Fellows — I have tried to get a rose to send you but all the flowers have been stripped from the gardens about here. If you can read this letter you will do extremely well. I never wrote so poorly in my life it seems to me. Accept my best wishes for your welfare. With much esteem

Your Friend
Ed Weller

Direct hereafter to the 20th instead of the 12th corps. The other direction the same as before.

From Bivouack of 107th N.Y.V.
Near *Ackworth, Ga.*
June 9th, 1864

Dear Friend Nett,

Your very interesting and encouraging letter of the 28th Ult. was thankfully received last evening. I had thought that I wrote you a letter after the Second battle we have had here, but on looking at my diary I find that I have not. Well, we passed through another battle on the 25th Ult, and one much fiercer and with much greater loss to our Regt. than the first ones, having lost in killed and wounded in our Regt. 152 officers and men. Comp. H. lost three men killed and thirteen wounded. Charley Duryea was wounded quite severely in the left shoulder but will recover without much trouble. He is now in the Hospital at Chattanooga. I presume he will get home as soon as his wound will permit. He is the only one with whom you are acquainted that was injured in our Regt.

One Co. of our Regt., Co. F lost all their commissioned officers and the Capt. and 1st Lieut. badly wounded. The Capt. has since died of his wounds. The 1st L. will recover I think. I am now commanding that Co. (F). I did not like the idea of leaving my own Co. but the Colonel was bound that I should take command of Co. F. so I acquiesed.

You can hardly imagine how much good it does me to receive and peruse your kind letter. No lady who writes such an incouraging and patriotic letter can be called anything but a true and noble hearted woman. One who values her country and its institutions with the highest esteem. Such letters do more to encourage the soldier in the field to do their duties bravely than anything else I can think of.

I am certainly very thankful that I have been preserved through all the battles in which I have been engaged. I have now passed through five very severe battles, besides several skirmishes. Allow me to thank you for your wishes for my welfare and I sincerely hope that your wishes and prayers for my safe return home may be heard and realized.

We have been encamped for two days here in breast-works facing the enemy — but no fighting has occured excepted occasionally a little picket fireing. We received orders last eve to prepare for a ten days march against the enemy and to start this morning — but orders came last night that we would not start this morning but probably sometime through the course of the day.

I expect to see considerable more hard fighting before this campaign is over. But I have every confidence in our success. This campaign will probably last yet this month when we shall rest for a few weeks. We are all pretty well fatigued out having been marching and fighting for nearly forty days now. I am getting quite thin in flesh but feel well and can eat my rations yet. This is, what I can get, which is not very extensive but plenty of such as it is.

I presume you would not recognise me now the same Ed Weller that I was when home as I am so bronzed and thined with the excessive heat and exposure of the southern sun and climate. We are having green peas, new potatos and apples when we can get out in the country to find them.

I had hardly dreamed that any of my friends in H. could take such an interest in my welfare as you seem to in mine and I hope with you that some time soon we may be permitted to exchange thoughts verbally instead of through the pen. Nothing would please me better. Oh, how much I would like to drop in and see you this morning as of old, in your morning working apparel, or even this eve and sit and have one of our old chats. How pleasing it would be — but we must bide time and trust in the future for the realization of our wishes.

Then Geo. Burge and Kate Mix are about being married. Well that is all right. Geo. will get a good woman, and Kate will get a very good fellow. The only objection is his very poor health. Then you think Bell and Hod will not make a hitch of it do you? . . . Do you remember the night Hod and Bell were at your home and I was there when the light was turned down pretty low and they lay on the floor in the corner? I have a little suspicion about that affair. Ahem — what say you, I thought you had at the time.

It is really too bad that there was no young fellows that you cared to invite up during the absence of Mr. and Mrs. Tracy. How I wish I might have been there, but then I might have been in the same fix that the young men that were there. But I think I should have run the risk.

How would you like to dine with me today. I am to have boiled pork and greens, hardtack, and coffee. Won't that be a sumtious repast. Every one can not afford such an extensive dinner. I have to put on some airs to afford it myself. But I must close. I have done extremely well for me. This is the longest letter I have written since I have been on this campaign. Hoping to hear from you very soon. I remain your sincere friend and well wisher.

Ed Weller

P.S. The name of the last battle in which we were engaged (the 25th May) is the Battle of Dallas Gap, Ga. Accept my sincere regards and love

Ed.

From the field, in front of Johnsons Army
Near *Marrietta, Ga.*
June 24th, 1864

Dear Friend Nettie,

Your letter of the 17th Inst. was received last evening and
as there is a mail going out this P.M. I will try and write you
a few lines. We are laying in our breastworks and entrenchments less than a mile from the Rebel army and facing
them. Have been here two days. On the 22nd we left our
other line of works and advanced on the Rebs — driving
them before us nearly two miles.

On reaching a high ridge running nearly north and south
on which we are now located and fortified, we halted and
formed line of battle and planted our artillery. Then commenced throwing up a line of breastworks to protect us
from the fire of the enemy in case they attacked us. We had
thrown up but a few pieces of timber and each before the
Rebs drove in skirmishers and came out of the woods in
four lines of battle to charge on us and the batteries.

They were obliged to cross a ravine and an open field
before they could get near enough so their fireing would do
us any harm. We did not wait till they got near us — but
opened on them as soon as they came out of the woods, with
artillery and infantry. The artillery throwing shell, grape
and cannister.

We had a splendid view of them, being on considerably
higher ground and poured a destructive fire into them.
They made several attempts to charge us — but were repulsed every time with heavy loss. This was just at sun-
down. As soon as it got dark they fell back to their works
and have not made an attempt to charge us since. I think

what they suffered in that fight will repay them in part for the damage they did us on the 25th Ult.

I walked over the battlefield the next morning and saw many of their dead they had left behind. Prisoners who have been captured since the fight state that they lost very heavy in those charges and carried off most their killed. We buried some fifty in front of our lines. We lost only two men in our Regt. one killed and one wounded. The loss in our Regiment since this campaign commenced will reach one hundred and seventy five (175) men.

I received a letter from Charley Duryea a few days ago. His wound is getting along finely. He is at Louisville, Ky. in General Hospital. Capt. Compton was not wounded but is quite sick back at the hospital.

Charley and George Caryell are also back at the hospital at Chattanooga. Fin Mitchell has lately been promoted to 1st Lieut. but is not yet mustered. We lay very near the 141st. All the Havana boys of that Regt. are well, I believe. I am yet in command of Co. F. of our Regt. Have lost since the battle of Dallas, in that Co. one killed and three wounded. Also three died of wounds received at Dallas.

Well I shall have to stop writing for a moment as my colored boy sayes dinner is ready. I have had my dinner and will resume my writing. We are living very high nowadays, have pork, hardtack and coffee for breakfast and of course for dinner coffee, hardtack, and pork for a change. Then for supper we have a little coffee, pork and fried hardtack. Occasionally when on the march we can get new potatoes, green peas, apples and blackberries. But when in the field can not get these things. You can readily see that I am in danger of getting the Gout on the account of so high living. Indeed I would be glad to sit down to one of your well prepared meals. I am very confident that I could do a good meals of victuals justice. And knowing your ability to get up a good dish of most anything, I know I could do it good justice.

I wrote you nearly two weeks ago, so you must not be disappointed if I do not give you much news in this. You say Leroy would not let you read the postscript of his letter. Well, I can not tell whether he did right or not as I do not now remember what the P.S. contained, but I hardly think it contained anything that I should object to your seeing.

I do think it is a very remarkable occurance that you young people dared to attempt to go out walking on Sunday. Has it not been talked up already around town, if it has not I shall begin to think H. is improving in the talking line. Then you girls have quit going to church for the purpose of having a beaux home, have you? I should think there ought to be young men enough in H. to see that the young ladies of the town were well taken care of.

If I were there, that, I should consider my first duty. I fear that you are too easily discouraged, Nett. Seem to think you girls will have to live a life of single blessedness if many more men are killed. I have heard many say that they preferred single life, but very few I see follow the doctrine however.

Then Frank T. is soon to be married is he? Please give him my regards and I will wish him much joy after the event of his marriage. Indeed I should think you would feel very sober over such an event, as this is the second one of your old beaux that has married within a year and you yet left out and not possessed of the one of (all the most sought for objects by young ladies), a Husband. But keep up good cheer Nett, your time is coming I presume.

Our mails are again regularly sent out and received by us. I was considerably surprised a few days ago at receiving the compliments and address of a young lady with whom I never was acquainted or ever saw. I have not yet answered it and do not know whether I shall. . . . Well, I must close. I have already written much more than I thought I would when I commenced. Heavy skirmishing is now going on in our front and we may have a fight before night. Bullets flying over my head while I sit here on a hardtack box writing. Give my kind regards to Mr. and Mrs. Tracy and all others who may inquire after me. Write soon. With high regards,

> I remain truely
> Your Friend
> Ed Weller

From Camp of 107th N.Y.V.
Near the *Cattahoochee River, Ga.*
July 15th, 1864

Dear Friend Nettie,

Your letter of the 2nd Inst. was just this moment received and perused. I was thinking of you this morning and made up my mind that it was nearly time I should receive a letter from you and behold it came. I assure you it was thankfully received and its contents carefully noted.

It seems you still have fully your share of labor to perform in the household of D. Tracy. I pity those who have to work over a hot stove this terrible hot weather. Especially if it is anywhere near as hot as it is here, which I very much doubt. I used to think I experienced some very warm weather north but it does not compare with the extreme hot weather we are having here now. During our late advance many officers and soldiers were sun struck. I came very near being sun struck one day when on the march but we stopped and bivouacked in a few moments after as fortune would have it.

We have now been in camp for about a week near the above named river. We are only about ten miles from Atlanta and can see the city very distinctly from a height near our camp. It looks like quite a large city from here. The Rebs are just across the river in the fortifications. We shall probably not cross until they are compelled by a flank movement of some kind, to evacuate their works and fall back. If we were to cross now we should endanger the lives of many men.

When we took possession of Marrietta, near here, we captured some four hundred women, who were at work in a factory making knapsacks and haversacks for the Rebel army. They are said to be a hard looking set of females by those who have seen them. A valuable capture I should judge. They are now fed and supported by the U.S. government.

I was on picket duty down on the bank of the river two or three days ago and while there saw lots of Rebs on the opposite bank. They conversed freely with our men and made an agreement with them to not shoot at each other that day. Consequently I had comparatively a quiet picket duty to what is usual when so near the enemy. Some of the men of both sides were in the river swimming together during the day, but they got rather too intimate in the latter part of the day and I was compelled to put a stop to it. All is quiet along the lines today. We expect to move every day. There has been some talk of our corps going back to the Army of the Potomac but I do not put any confidence in the report. . . .

You asked me how I should spend the 4th. That memorable day was spent by me on the battle field in our entrenchments. I should not have known that it was the fourth by what was transpiring about me. Had I not been reminded of it by the sudden striking up of our brass bands early in the morning playing all the national airs. It was perfectly splendid to hear all the bands of the Army of the Cumberland playing along the whole line.

How was it, did not some gallant young man invite you to ride out that day? Surely some nice fellow ought to have given so agreeable a young lady as you an invitation to ride out with him. I certainly should had I been there. I certainly do distinctly remember the 4th of two years ago and the plesant time I had on that occasion. I was wishing on the 4th of this month to Lieut W. of my company that I was where I was two years ago. I have a distinct memory of our coming so near upsetting that night. Those were happy days. There has no doubt been quite a change in society within the past two years in Havana. I could see quite a change when I was there — but if nothing happens to me I shall be at home a year from now to again enjoy the sweet society of parents and friends. . . .

I am glad to hear that Leroy is getting along well in H. but do really hope he will not get connected with a certain class of society which I could name, there. You must bring him to strict account for all his wrong acts and sayings or if you will inform me of his misdoings I will correct the chap for I do not want him to depart from the path of rectitude in the least. I suppose he eclipses me in gayety by far. Hope he will not go too far. Next time you write me I want you to give me the misdoings of my worthy brother you refer to.

It is really too bad that you could not have had the arms of a man instead of Morpheus to have thrown yourself into.

I think I would have been just the man to have been present on that night you speak of. You are indeed the same Nett you used to be. I can see no change. How gladly would I drop in and spend the evening if I were where I could. Am sure I could enjoy an evening in your agreeable society. Hope I may ere long have that privilege too. . . .

Well, I guess I will close this scribbling for it is nothing else and if you can make out half I have written you will do extremely well. . . .

Ever Your Friend,
Ed Weller

In the trenches
Near *Atlanta, Ga.*
August 13th, 1864

Dear Friend Nettie,
    Your letter of the 2nd Inst. was recieved yesterday. I was happy (as usual) to hear from you. How well I shall succeed in writing you much of a letter this time I shall leave you to judge. I have been quite unwell for nearly a week but am now feeling quite like myself again. Was threatened with fever—had a very severe attack of Colic and second night after I was taken sick and had to have the surgeon with me nearly all night. This is the first sickness I have had since entering upon this campaign. Think I shall come out all right however.
    We are now farely established in the siege of Atlanta. Have build heavy entrenchments in front of the Rebel works in which we are obliged to keep pretty close for fear of getting hit by Rebel sharp shooters who are located in their forts and houses near their lines. Scarcely a day passes

by but that we have one or more men killed or wounded here in our works. Several have given me pretty close calls but a miss is as good as a mile (as the saying is).

We can see the city of Atlanta from our forts and entrenchments — quite plainly. Our heavy canon are throwing shell into Atlanta every day. We can hear them burst in the place from here. It must make it pretty uncomfortable for the southern shivellry and aristocracy of that place. My opinion is that we shall have a long and tedious siege here before taking the place. We are almost under the portholes of the Reb forts.

There is an artillery duel between the two sides nearly every day and quite often they throw shell and solid shot into our works. Then is the time we have to lay low. We have been quite fortunate however and not had many men killed or wounded by shell. We are constantly building new works up closer to those of the enemy. Heavy skirmishing is now going on between our pickets and the rebs and the bullets are whistling over my head as I write but I am bound to finish this letter notwithstanding. We are having considerable wet weather here now which makes our trenches a very uncomfortable place to stay.

I have got a heavy breast work built around my quarters which are located under a huge walnut tree. They are by far the most plesant and comfortable quarters in the Regt. I have many and frequent visits from the other officers of the Regt. and we have some quite gay and festive times among ourselves telling stories and getting off jokes on each other.

I received a letter from Charley Duryea a few days ago. He gave me a full account of his visit to Havana and especially the eve he and Leroy were at your house. I judge you must have had a gay time. Charley spoke quite highly of Miss Fellows, but thought she was not as well posted of the "tight holt" as you. He sayes you have not changed at all in that respect. I am having one of my old fashioned tooth aches today and fear I shall be obliged to delay finishing this letter till it gets easier for tooth aches is a bad thing to have when writing a letter and make it at all interesting.

Well, I have been to dinner and my teeth have become easier and I will make another trial at writing. The weather is very warm here yet, but not so uncomfortable as it has been. We now have cool breezes every day which is much more plesant than the extreem heat. You must not get discouraged Nett in regard to the final result of this war. There will no doubt be many more lives given up as a sacrafice on the Alter of Freedom before this strife shall end but believe me when I say that the supremacy of this glorious and free government will be maintained and this wicked rebellion put down, and those who survive the contest will enjoy the blessings of a free and happy country.

I should like to have been present with you on the night Charley was there. I have no doubt I should have taken a drink of milk punch with you and what else I should have done I can not say. . . .

It is really too bad that you were obliged to give up your Pic-Nic party on account of rain on the day refered to. I should like to be present with you with you have another excursion to Cayuga Lake—but doubt whether I could interest you so much better than the partner you spoke of that was to accompany you. Mr. Vail you know, possesses greater conversational powers than your humble servant, and then I could not expect to support quite as gay a rig as he.

Charley Durkee is here in my tent, just came over to see me. He is looking well, and is the same Charley as ever. I am also glad to hear that you have made the misunderstanding between you and Leroy all right. I always knew brother L. to be a great lover of the ladies society and it is so with all my brothers but you know there must always be an odd sheep in every flock and Ed is the odd one. So that you know that accounts for my tastes in regard to the ladies. I have no doubt but that many of you young ladies see many lonesome young men north considerable. However I hope Havana may escape the draft and fill their quota by enlistment. When I hear of these drafts I feel glad than I am in the service and my time so near out. If I can only escape as well as I have so far, I shall be among you again within another year.

I am now acting Adjutant of our Regt. while our Adjutant is absent on business for a week or two. . . . But I must close, Write soon.

Your sincere friend,
Ed

Sunday morn — 8 A.M.

I could not mail this yesterday so will add a little. I am feeling first rate this morning and feel very much like going to hear a good sermon preached somewhere. I should like to walk into the Presbyterian church at H. and listen to one of Mr. Chesters interesting sermons this morning, but I am doomed to listen only to the booming of canon and whistling of bullets this holy sabbath. I am sorry to hear of your brother Charley fareing so hard. I do not think the officers of his Regt. are very good commisarys or they would get enough if it was in the country. Our Regt. never have been brought down to that yet.

Give my kind regards to Miss Fellows and say to her that I should be very much pleased to receive her photograph and the specimen of her hand writing also. But I must close as my duties call me down to HeadQuarters for a while. My regards to Mr. and Mrs. Tracy and others. Write soon.

Your Friend, Ed w.

P.S. Enclosed I send you a southern Lilly which I picked in a yard near here. I never saw one of this color north

Ed.

From Camp of 107th N.Y.V.
On the banks of the *Cattahoochee River, Ga.*
August 29th, 1864

My Dear Friend Nett,

Your letter of the 13th Inst. was received nearly a week ago and I assure you I was most happy to peruse another of your excellent epistles. I have no correspondent whose letters are hailed with as much pleasure as yours.

You will see by the heading of my letter that we are again located on the banks of the Cattahoochee River. We are quite nicely located on the heights on the south side of the river over looking it and the valley through which it flows. We are guarding a large R.R. bridge and ford across the river. Our whole corps is scattered along the river guarding fords and our lines of communication.

We left the front of Atlanta on the night of the 25th Inst. and fell back to this place to guard our communications while the remainder of this "Grand Army" started off on a decisive movement against the city of Atlanta which if successful will compel the Rebs to abandon the city and go out and fight Gen'l Shermans invincable Army. And believe me, if they attack him they will get the worst threashing they have ever had for Genl. Sherman has got a splendid army with him and have taken twenty days rations with them so they will not be dependent on a line of communications.

We consider ourselves quite lucky in being the corps chosen to come here to guard this point. It is a very important position and needs troops that have had experience in the field. You can hardly imagin how strange it seems to me to get out of hearing of the booming of canon and the whizing of bulletts about me once more. It is indeed a grand change. And when I tell you that I have gained so much flesh since coming here that yesterday when putting on my belt and sword, I was obliged to let out my belt about two inches in order to get it around me, you will readily see how much good it is doing me to get out of the constant excitement and noise of the battlefield. I have had very comfortable quarters built for myself and mess which consists of three officers beside myself. We have some gay times together I assure you. . . .

You seem to have much anxiety for my safety and fear that my time will yet come. That is very true Nett, my time may yet come, but I have one consolation that if called upon to die or suffer from severe wounds it will be in the defense of our union and a cause that should prompt every loyal man to aid in its furtherance.

I certainly highly prize your interest in my welfare and it shall always be remembered by me as coming from one of my very best friends. On the other hand I very often think of you and the many plesant hours I have spent in your society, and wish you all the happiness and success in life that is possible. . . .

In your answer to my enquiring of what you thought of my reinlisting for three years longer, you do not seem to encourage it very much and think me entitled to a good long rest. That is very true, I think myself that I am, or shall be, when my three years is up, entitled to a good rest. But when I get to thinking about this acursed rebellion I am almost temted to volunteer my services to the U.S. as long as there is a rebellion in existance. But according to the late order from the War Department we are not allowed to reinlist until our time is within two months of being out and I can assure you, our Regt. will never reinlist under such circumstances. Consequently you can look for the 107th N.Y. home in about ten months. If we can only get through summer safely, I shall have hopes of getting home again. I do think it rather spoils one of us soldiers to go home on a visit. The parting from friends and perhaps never to see them again is a sad thought. My being home last summer made me feel very lonesome for a while after I returned to the Regt. Still it did me a great deal good. . . .

I think it would seem very good indeed to Daniel to be sole proprietor of the store. I am certain it would to me if in like circumstance. I wish him the best of success in all his business enterprises. Tell Miss Fannie F. that owing to late orders from HeadQrs. I have given up reinlisting and if spared to get home, shall do my best to attend to the wants of the young ladies. I hardly think I shall be very good in the Arm service when I get home as I am getting very much out of practice and fear shall lose all liking for that once to me, pleasant duty. I have no doubt you all need more experience in this branch of the service — oh yes, of course you do — Ahem. To be certain. But I must bid you an affectionate good night as it is bed time and I am quite tired out., writing so steadily today getting out my company reports. Good night and pleasant dreams.

Your friend,
Ed.

7

Camp of 107th N.Y. Vols.
Atlanta, Georgia
Sept. 15th, 1864

Dear Friend Nett,

Your letter of the 5th Inst. was welcomely received yesterday and I improve this early opportunity to reply, fearing if I delay it, I shall not have another chance for several days in succession. Our regiment is now doing duty in the city and find it much more plesant than marching and fighting I assure you.

I see by your letter that you have received the news north of the taking of Atlanta. We took possession of it on the 2nd Inst. The 107th N.Y. has the honor of being one of the first Regiments to enter the city, on the morning of that day. Gen'l Slocum who is now commanding our Corps ordered a reconnoissance toward Atlanta and the Regts. selected were the 123rd N.Y., 117th, 102nd Ill., and a squad of cavalry all under the command of Colonel Crane of our Regt.

We left camp at 4 A.M. and in reaching the Rebel works found them evacuated and marched direct into the city. The remainder of our Corps came up that night. We found the city badly riddled by our shot and shell. There was scarcely a dwelling or business house in the main part of the place but that was pierced by them and some families had a cave dug in their gardens, floored, carpeted and furnished for living in. Many of them told me that they actually lived in those caves during the shelling of the city by our siege guns. It was quite a curiousity to visit those caves soon after we occupied the city and see with what taste and comfort they had arranged them for living in.

Most of the citizens that remained in the place, were out at the gates and on the walks to see the Yankees come in, and viewed us with seeming curiosity. They expected no doubt to see a huge set of beings but I rather think they came to the conclusion that we were human, in appearance at least.

A majority of those I saw were ladies. Many of them waved their white handkerchiefs at us very politely while some few swung to the breeze the stars and stripes which were cheered enthusiasticly by our boys as we passed. I saw some fine looking young ladies among them and I think I shall make it a point to form their acquintance as soon as possible. I have not had time, since g since getting rested out and my company matters settled up, to make any calls, but I must find time soon.

The Rebels destroyed a vast amount of stores here when they left and everything denoted that they had left in a great hurry. It was one of the proudest days of my life when I marched through the city of Atlanta at the head of my company, and to think that we had compelled old Hood to evacuate this strong hold and fine city, thus ending our summer campaign.

Our whole Army is now encamped (with the exception of our corps) outside the city some nine miles. Our corps is located about the city. The whole army is to rest out for a month, clothe up, receive pay, and prepare for a vigorous winters campaign at the end of that time.

We arrested some three hundred Rebels in different parts of the city who had secreted themselves — doubtless intending to change their uniform for a citizens suit, and remain here. But we were rather too soon for them and gobbled them up before they had time to do much changing of clothes. We arrested a Rebel Captain in the act of changing his uniform for a citizens suit, he was not allowed to make any further changes in his toilet — but put his little bundle of clothes under his arm and was marched off under guard.

We are encamped on a beautiful green in the city near the Macon R. R. depot; have a fine camp and have got everything arranged as comfortable as we could wish. Myself and comrads (officers of Co. H.) have the best quarters in camp, and you will probably be somewhat surprised when I tell you that our quarters are furnished with sofa. chairs, a nice book case and writing table, and a good large dining table and we are expecting to have mattresses to sleep on in a day or two. This is all captured property from deserted Rebel houses.

I tell you it seems like civilization to seat myself in a sofa chair once more, and as I write I am seated in a sofa chair

OVERLEAF   The Home Front. *The original caption on this photo of Havana, New York, taken in 1863, labels it "Reading the Civil War News," referring to the three figures grouped left foreground. The new Montour House, left, was host to the Welcome Home banquet when the war ended. One of the crinolined figures, center, is identified as Antoinette Watkins' sister, Mrs. Woodhull. In 1895 Havana's name was changed to Montour Falls, after the falls visible in the background.*

and one of my feet in another. So you may readily conclude
that I am well situated for a soldier that has been through
the rough scenes that I have during the past six months. . . .

I am glad to hear that you remain so firm to the cause of
our country, and would not hurrah for McClellen, it surely
shows your patriotism, and that you uphold the cause for
which your brother and friends are fighting for. McClellen
is nought here in the army. It is all old Abe. He is the man
for the times and the one who should have the settling of
this trouble, and mind you, he is our next president if we
soldiers have any say in the matter.

I have but just got over my illness and begin to feel like
Ed again. Hope I shall have no more such attacks. That was
the first one since I entered the army, and I hope will be the
last, yet (as you say) I have been very fortunate to escape as
well as I have, considering the hardships I have endured.

I am glad to hear that Bell and Hod are living so cosily
and wish them all the happiness thru life that is possible.
Nett, I heard some news the other day by the way of a letter, and yet I do not know as I can consider it news either,
and I will tell you, as you told me some time ago, of what
you heard of my affairs. It is this — that you were engaged to
Mr. Vail and was to be married sometime this month, now
what you think? It was told me by a person who pretended
to know of the whole arrangements etc.

Allow me, Nett, in advance of the finale scene which will
make you both one, to congratulate you on your success,
hoping that you may be equally as fortunate through life
and joy and happiness be your lot. Ha, Ha, Ha. What a
world of gossip this is. Who won't they have you engaged
and married to, but it really seems to me that you ought to
be able to select and secure one from out the large number

of suiters that Madam Rumer has had you engaged to. I
shall soon begin to think that you a real flirt.

I also heard that one or two other young ladies of H. were
meditating the same thing. I judge the young ladies of H.
must be getting tired of single life: it is but natural, however, that they should. I fear us poor soldiers will stand a
slim chance when this cruel war is over if the girls all get
such notions in their heads.

I must tell you what I am to have for dinner today. Roast
Pig, potatoes, bread, (butter is out of the question) pickled
onions, coffee and for desert apple dumplings. This we
think is a very huge dinner here but if I were at home I
should not think so much of it. I used to think, very often,
when on the march, or rather, wished I could sit down to
once of your bountifully spread tables prepared by your
hands; it would have been relished well, I assure you. . . .

But I must close as I fear I have written much already
that will not interest you; but you know what a long
winded fellow I am, so will excuse all imperfections etc.
Write soon—remember me to Daniel and wife and family.
With kindest regards to yourself, I am as ever your friend,

Ed

From Office of A.R.Q.M. — 107th N.Y.V.
Mitchell Street, *Atlanta, Ga.*
Oct. 15th, 1864

My Dear friend Nett,

Your very welcome and interesting letter was received today and knowing or at least supposing you would be glad to hear from me immediately, I improve this beautiful moon-light evening in replying to your letter.

We have been deprived of a mail for three weeks till today, on account of the R.R. being destroyed by the Rebs between this city and Nashville. Communication is now open again however, and I hope will remain so in the future; for I assure you it seems really very lonely to be deprived of letters from home and friends. I was extremely lucky today as regards mail. Got six letters and quite a number of papers. Do you not think me in luck? You will readily see my appreciation of your letter as it is the first of the six that I answer tonight. The others I shall lay by for another day.

You will see by the heading of my letter that I have again changed my position in the army and I presume you will wonder, not being acquainted with military initials what those letters designate. I will explain.

I believe I was in command of the city mounted patrols at my last writing; in two or three days after, I was offered by Colonel Cane of our Regt. a much better position. So I resigned command of the patrols and accepted it.

It is Acting Regimental Quartermaster of 107th, in place of Lt. Howard who is detailed in the Quarter master Department of the Army of the Cumberland. In my present position I have charge of drawing and issueing all clothing, rations and other stores required by the Regt. I have a horse and equipments, two assistants, a commissary and quartermasters Sergeant. They are required to do most of the heavy business and I see that it is done right etc. I have a Head Quarters wagon etc. to carry my things in, and when on a campaign I am not required to be in battles, but remain to the rear with the supply trains and see that everything due the Regt. is furnished promptly.

I sometimes think I had rather be with the Regt. and my company enduring the hardships with them, but then I have made up my mind that I have seen nearly all the active field service that I wish to. I have already passed through ten hard fought battles and come out unharmed. I hope with you that I may be equally as fortunate during the next ten months. Yes, less than ten months has yet to pass and then I am a citizen again if God in his providence shall spare me.

All the army except our Corps has left this vicinity and gone back on the R.R. as the Rebel army are trying to sever our communications and compel us to evacuate the city. But Gen'l Sherman does not propose to do any such thing. He has gone back with the rest of the army and has already had one or two heavy fights with them and defeated them every time. It is thought that our Corps will remain here to hold and garrison the city all winter. Everything seems to indicate it here at present.

I must tell you how nicely I am located in my new position. I have an office in a nice little white house on Mitchell street in the main part of the city. I have what was used by the family who lived here as a parlor, for my office and a bed room opening from it as a sleeping apartment. The other rooms in the house are used for HeadQrts. of the Col. and staff. My furniture consists of a bureau, bookcase, and small library, a nice mahogany center chair, one large arm chair, my business desk and table. There is a nice grate in my office for burning coal in: so you see I am almost as comfortably situated as if I were at home. The nicest of the whole thing is there is a fine looking young lady living next door from my office. She plays the piano and sings beautifully, my ears are greeted with sweet music for my evening.

Gen'l Sherman has compelled nearly all the citizens of the city to leave and go either north or south as he wished to use the city wholly for military purposes. There is but few ladies left here and I must say but a very few that I care to make the acquaintance of. All the most wealthy and prominent people have left and I hear today that my lady friend next door intends to go north with her mother and brother next week. How much I shall miss her — Ahem. I am messing here with the Col, Major, and adjutant. We have everything as nice as soldiers could wish.

I received a letter from Leroy and Charly Harris today. You may tell Leroy I will answer his letter in a very few days. I am glad to know that you think it no task, but rather a pleasure to write me. And Nett, you write me such good letters that I must say they contain more items of interest to me than any one with whom I ever corresponded. And as we both seem to prize each others letters with the same interest we must necessarily be good mutual friends, which I consider we are?

You say you have sometimes feared that you expressed too much anxiety for me. I do not see why you should keep it back if you really felt such an anxiety for my welfare, for you know we have always interchanged thoughts and opinions as freely as if we had been acquainted since childhood. Do not refrain, Nett, from saying anything you wish to when ever you write me. Always feel assured that whatever you write me is thankfully received.

You doubtless remember my writing in one of my letters to you that I had sometimes thought it might be that I entertained too much friendship for you—fearing it was unbidden. And do you remember the answer you gave me? I do perfectly well, and often think of it. So whenever you begin to surmise you are expressing too much interest in my welfare, just think of the answer you gave me and remember Nett, that you can never feel more interest in my welfare than I do in yours, and that I am true to what I say to you always; that is if written or spoken in an earnest way, I sometimes write in a jesting manner, but know that you are well enough acquainted with my way of writing to distinguish between the two.

I am very glad to hear that you and Leroy are on such good terms. Hope you may always remain such. Leroy is one of my best brothers if there is any best among them. He was always of a very social disposition, rather different from his brother Ed, don't you think so? I wish I might be with you again this year during the Institute, but it cannot be, so I shall have to be content here. Yes, I was with you just about a year ago. I remember very well shaking off the peaches from that tree back of the house, and you picked them up. I at the time eating almost as many as you picked up, I judge. I shall not have that pleasure this year. . . .

You ask me if I shall be home this winter. I shall if I can in any way obtain a leave of absence, and I hear that it is the intention of Gen'l Sherman to grant furloughs this winter. I should like to go home this winter dearly and see my relatives and friends. I do not doubt for a moment Nett, but that you would do all in your power to make my visit pleasant. I have that confidence in you and know I should enjoy a visit with you very much indeed.

I very often allow myself to picture a bright and happy

future dawning in the distance for me but have for a long
time refrained from revealing it for fear of the results. Yes,
my dear friend, I have thought and hoped that we may yet
become nearer than mere confidential friends. Yet such a
hope may aught I know, be hopeless. But I trust not. We
have been friends long enough to know each others hearts
and feelings pretty well, I am quite sure you can not but
know mine, and I have reason to believe that we know each
others quite well, but I will say no more on this subject at
present. . . .

Now Nett, about that startling news, as you call it, that I
heard some time ago in regard to your soon being married
to a Mr. V. did you presume to suppose I believed such a
story for a moment? I hope not, for I never did. And as for
my calling you a flirt, I did it, but only in a jest. I did not
think you would consider I meant what I said when I made
such an assertation and I can not believe you did.

As regards the source of such intelligence, I presume you
may guess pretty close who gave it, but the one I think you
refer to is not the person who gave me this information. But
the person you refer to has occasionally written me items in
regard to you, but she is blameless this time. As for Call and
Marinda, they very seldom write me town gossip, but that
which is currently rumered throughout town — they say.
Marinda, I do not correspond with now, have not for six
months, it is no pleasure to correspond with persons who do
not answer you letters only once in three months.

I will tell you one thing Nett, which you may or may not
be aware of, and that is you have one or two enemies in H.
—probably pretended friends at your face, who watch all
your movements and sayings and several times have attempted to prejudice me against you by writing some of

your doings etc. I have never yet said a word in return to their allusions to such matters, and do not intend to. All they have or can ever say will not make me think any less of you. I know I have some few enemies in H. and I presume I have to take agoing over by such friends occasionally, away off here in the Army — but let them talk, Nett. Our shoulders are broad and can bear considerable.

I recollect very well our conversation on the subject of marriage etc. when riding from Cayuga Lake once and then you assured me of the same thing as you do now. It takes but very little to start a story in Havana. Enclosed I send you a Reb love letter I found soon after our occupation of the city. I found it the next day after it was written. You will find it a gay thing.

Nett, I think you owe me another letter. It is hardly fair you know to try to get off with writing me but one letter to my two. So I consider you indebted to me one letter but I must close as I have already written such a long letter that I fear you will tire of it before you are through reading it.

My kind regards to Mr. and Mrs. Tracy and others. Write as soon as you receive this, and direct the same as usual, and believe me ever your sincere Friend,

Ed.

P.S. Nett, tell Daniel that I am getting to be a great politician and am working like a hero in the Regt. to gain as many votes for old Abe as possible. I intend to send my vote to Havana to be put in. I am extremely sorry to see so little patriotism displayed north in the coming Presidential Election. In my opinion the question is union or disunion. If Lincoln and Johnson are elected we may look for an honorable peace—but if little McC. gains the Presidential chair, this war so far is of no avail. But I hope for the best results and readily give three hearty cheers for Lincoln and Johnson.

Ed.

From Office of A.R.Q.M. 107th N.Y. Vols.
Atlanta, Ga.
Oct. 25th, 1864

My Dear Friend, Nettie,

I wrote you just ten days ago, but this evening being alone in my office, the other officers having gone down street and feeling a little lonely, my thoughts naturally soared to the distant north, and, my dear friends there and I concluded to write you a few lines. Another reason I had for writing. I feared you might not receive the other letter, as our communications were so much interrupted by raids of the enemy. But I am sure you will not object in the least to receiving another letter from me for it you are at all like me, the oftener you receive letters from friends the better it pleases you.

We received another large mail a day or two ago but I was not quite as fortunate in the way of letters as before. I am enjoying myself as well as a soldier can. Have nice quarters and plenty of fun; that is, among the officers. I was, a moment ago, trying to bring to mind what I wrote in my

Edwin Weller as a lieutenant (1864)

last letter so that I should not repeat too much of its contents, but I can not think of all.

I have received accounts of the grand weddings of Miss
Sarah Vail and Miss Marinda McMillan through Mrs. Hin-
man and Charly Duryea both. I really think Marinda has
gone and done it now. I had heard considerable about her
and Eli keeping company etc. but hardly supposed that she
would be so unfeeling, as to break a former engagement and
that to a poor soldier boy, and marry such a fellow as Eli
Dunham. I am really surprised to hear it. I saw Charley
Durkee last Sunday, he was over to my office to see me and
I had a long talk with him in regard to the matter. He
seemed to be very much surprised that she should make
such a move but seemed to take it in good cheer and said
that he was glad to be rid of her, if that was the kind of
fickle person she had become.

I admire Charleys pluck in the matter. He sayes to me,
Ed, there is plenty more North who are as good as she, if
not a little better, for me. I do not know but that she has
done well, but can not see it with the present light I have
got on the subject. Any young lady who is engaged to a soldier, and jilts him for a stay-at-home, I am a little inclined to
be down on. But I will say no more on that case. . . .

I believe you sent me word through Charley in regard to
you and Mr. V. and that I must not believe all I hear. I assure you Nett, I really did not believe it when I first heard
the rumer. I was thoroughly posted long since in regard to
the talking propensities of a majority of the inhabitants of
H. consequently I gave no credence to the report. If you
should receive my other letter you will fully understand my
opinion of the thing and of my sentiments toward you. I
expressed sentiments in that letter which I never did before

to any other young lady, and felt at the same time what I wrote.

I hope Nett, you will think seriously of the connection as regards our future lives, I have always said that I would marry no young lady, however rich or accomplished she might be, unless I loved her with all my heart. It is not my purpose to merely get a partner in life, to keep house or to attend to the kitchen, but I want one whom I can love in the full sense of the word. And Nett you may have many times thought I was rather a singular person in regard to such things and a long while in coming to the object, but it is for this reason.

I have always thought I would make no demonstrations in that direction while I was in the Army, as I did not wish to have any young ladies prospects injured by such a thing, in case I was killed or crippled for life. But during the past few months I have been gradually changing my mind in that direction.

Before I came into the Army I esteemed you very highly as a friend, but our associations and correspondence since then have very much strengthened and increased that es- teem. And now Nett I can say with truth and sincerity that I love you. And I must say I have reason to think that it is mutual, at least I hope so. In your answer to this, I want you if you please, to give me your opinions and feelings on the matter. And if you can consistantly, with your view on the matter, give me a reply, I should be very glad to receive it.

There is one thing which I wish to tell you, and that is, if Charley D. or any other person ever tells you anything that I have written them in regard to you, you need not put much of any confidence in it. Charley has lately been trying to draw me on and if possible find out my opinion of you. I have generally given him quite a mixed up idea of thing, as though I had no intentions that way and he still persists in the thing.

Now I have a presentment that Fanny and he are trying to get something out of me, and I do not care to tell them just what I think, for I fear it would soon be in the mouths of the gossipers of H. If Fanny ever sayes anything about the matter or anything I have ever written Charley — pass the thing off as well as you can.

There is a lady in H. (and I presume you can guess who she is) often trys to get me to acknowledge something and often writes to me about you, but I give her no satisfactory reply. I have got a great deal to tell you if I ever get home, and I hope to this winter, which may somewhat surprise you. I can not write half of it nor explain it so well in a letter, as I could if I were sitting by your side on that old familiar sofa at Daniels, and telling you in my usual way.

There is a rumer here today that our corps is going to be relieved, and going back near Chattanooga, I can not vouch for the truth of the report however. Well, I shall be obliged to close as the boys are coming in from down town and will bother me so I can not write. They are always raising Ned around. So I bid you an affectionate good night. Write soon and remember you owe me three letters now.

Your Ever affct. Friend,
Edd Weller

P.S. I have just received orders that I have to go out on a foraging expedition some twenty miles south of here, in charge of our brigade train. Shall probably have a gay time. Shall be gone four or five days.

Morning of 26th — I leave at 6 o'c., my train is ready and waiting me so I must go.

Good bye,
Ed

From *Atlanta, Ga.*
Nov. 8th, 1864

Dear Friend Nettie,

I have already written you two letters and have received no answer as yet from them; but I am not going to be so particular as to wait for an answer from every letter of mine, before writing you. This may be the last time you will hear from me in some time, perhaps a month or more. We are under marching orders and expect to move any day, and I understand the last mail leaves here today. Consequently I thought it best to improve the opportunity as it might be the last I shall have in some time.

We are going on an expedition south and off from the railroad where we will be deprived of a mail. Nevertheless, Nett, I want you to write me as often as your time will admit, perhaps they may reach me by courier line, and I will write you as often as there is any chance of sending a mail through.

My opinion is that Atlanta is to be evacuated when we move. I had hoped that we might be permitted to enjoy our comfortable quarters here this winter but it is not to be so it seems. I assure you I am quite loathe to leave my neat little office to endure the hardships of another hard campaign and especially at this time of the year. The weather is quite warm here at present but it is becoming the time of year when there is a great deal of storm weather in this southern climate. Our destination is not known for a certainty. Many conjecture however that we are bound for Mobile or Savannah. If so you probably will hear from me next time by the way of water via New York.

I attended the theatre in town last evening for the last time in this city, as the Troupe leave for Chattanooga today.

I received a note from Leroy day before yesterday. He stated that you were well and the rest of the good people of H.

The prospects do not appear very flattering at present for my getting home this winter. Yet I shall try hard to go, if we get anywhere, so I can get transportation. There is one consolation, however, that I have but nine months more to serve before I can go and stay. The time is wearing away fast. God grant that ere my time expires this acursed Rebellion may be put down. I feel anxious to be present at its last final struggle and witness with pleasure its last gasping breath.

I think of you often Nett and look forward with anxiety to the time when I can meet you again. I really hope I may hear from you before we leave this place, for when we start I shall consider all prospects gone, that I shall hear from you for some time. But I shall be obliged to close as the mail boy is awaiting my letter to carry out. Remember me kindly to Mr. and Mrs. Tracy and famlily. With best wishes for your welfare and much Love. I remain your true and sincere friend

Ed Weller

From *Atlanta, Ga.*
Nov. 11th, 1864

My Dear Friend Nettie,

Your very interesting letter of the 31st Oct. has just reached me and I was considerably puzzeled to know how I could get a letter through to you as there is no more mail sent from here through the mail department. But very luckily for me I came across a friend a few moments ago, who is going to Nashville this evening, and kindly offered to take a letter for me, and mail it at Nashville. So I improve the opportunity to write you.

There is no one else who I should take so much pains to get a letter through to, as you. I wrote you but a few days ago, when our last mail went out, informing you that we were about to march. We have remained here much longer than we expected and shall not leave I think before next week. I do not expect to have another opportunity to write you in a month or more, as the expedition on which we are going will be through the south where we shall have no communications.

But be assured Nett, that I shall write you at the very first opportunity that occurs and I do not want you to fail to write often as you can as your letters may reach me sooner than I expect and I shall always feel very anxious to hear from you.

I have just been over to the 141st. Saw Bryon who has just returned, promoted to Lieut. He is looking first rate. Also Lt. Mitchell and Coryell are well.

Nett, I never have received a letter that brought news of so much interest to me as yours, which I have just read. You will ere this fully know my sentiments in regard to you as I have written you two letters and explained my feelings on

the subject of our friendship as well as I could. But I want
to tell you something more in regard to what Charley may
tell you, or Miss Fellows. Charley has always thought, and
endeavored to know all my little secrets about such matters,
he has on several occasions asked me, my opinion of you,
and plainly showed a desire to know and in fact thought
that it was his perfect right to know my regards for you.

I have in every instance succeeded in making him believe
that I was entirely uninterested in you and that I had no intentions of becoming more than I was then, a friend. Yet I
have always said to him that if I were to select a partner for
life from the young ladies of Havana, I would select you in
preference to any other among them. But at the same time I
would tell him that the subject of matrimony was very far
from my mind, and I went so far as to make a bet with him
on which of us would be married or engaged first.

I have undoubtedly said many other things to him all of
which were intended for a blind, which I do not now
remember, but never anything against you in the least. He
has written me considerable about you since he has been at
home, but I make but very little reply to his questions etc. I
am confident of one fact and that is that Miss F. tells him
very much in regard to our matters, and he has undoubtedly told her all I have ever said, and I should not be
surprised if he colored them to suit his taste. I will sometime show you a letter which he wrote me in regard to you
and your affairs with Mr. V.

Yes, Nett we would both feel much different toward each
other, if we were to believe all we hear but I do not pretend
to believe anything except that which I know to be true. I
have long since learned, how much confidence to put in
what comes to me through certain sources in H. I am highly
pleased with your frankness in regard to your affairs with

Mr. V. and can not blame you for your inclinations to accept his offer, and do not know that I could have blamed you if you had taken one step further.

As I know I have not given you encouragement that I ought until lately, of more than a friendly nature. Yet Nett you little know what my opinions has been, and how often I have been on the very eve of telling you all, but as I wrote you in a previous letter, I had feared that it was not right to get a matter of so much importance to me and you also, settled to a certainty for fear that I might be taken away in fighting the battles of our country, and leave one to mourn my loss, and perhaps be the cause of blighting prospects which might otherwise have been realized. But Nett I have changed my opinion somewhat on that point.

I have always thought very highly of you indeed, since I left home, and more especially since my sojourn home last fall. If you remember the evening we were together after Mr. and Mrs. Tracy had retired one evening, I was on the point of telling you my sentiments toward you that night and can hardly tell you why I did not—but I put it off and have kept putting it off till of late.

I think now you fully understand my feelings. And to be frank I will say Nett that there is no one in this wide world whom I esteem as highly as you. I love you and Nett if you are willing to risk your destiny, fortune, happiness and all lifes cares and troubles with me—it shall be my aim through life always to make our lives one of happiness and pleasure. I am sure that you will do fully your share in that direction. I have every confidence in you and shall always expect you to write me your every care and trouble that I may in part share them with you. . . .

Nett, what is Daniels and Louises opinion of me and what do you think their advaice would be to you if you were to consult them in regard to our matters. I think I know about what Daniels opinion of me is but as for Louise, I have not the slightest idea. Please tell me if you consult them what their opinion of the matter is. I should really like to know. I shall be obliged to close as it is nearly train time and this must be in the hands of the friend who takes it for me within half an hour. Don't fail to write often and I will do the same. Nett I shall always be ready to answer any questions in regard to myself or anything you have heard, that should be explained at any time. May God bless and protect you from all afflictions and harm is the wish of your best friend on earth.

Ed

P.S. Please excuse this scribbling, as I have been compelled to write in great haste to get it ready in time and if it should be slightly disconnected you will attribute it to the haste in which I wrote. I would like to have had time to have written you a good long letter and think I could have made it more interesting but this will have to suffice this time and I will do better next time. Remember me to Mr. and Mrs. Tracy and family. With much love I bid you an affectionate farewell for the present.

Ed.

8

In many respects Sherman's march to the sea was the most daring, dramatic event of the war. Throughout the summer he had led his army slowly from Chattanooga to Atlanta, fighting a skillful but conventional war against a foe of declining power. Hood's forces were no match and gradually he yielded central Georgia, struggling to keep his dwindling troops as an integrated force-in-being.

With Atlanta finally secured, Sherman measured his own strength with a calculating eye and took a supreme risk. He decided to cut loose from all the usual supply sources and avenues of reinforcement and make a dash for Savannah and the coast where the sea-lanes would provide communication with the north. To do it, his Army would live off the land. If successful, the dash would again chop off a big piece of the Confederacy, and then he could turn northward heading toward a conjunction with Grant's Army of the Potomac.

One Confederate general, grasping the audacity of the plan as its outlines grew clear, commented that no commander had succeeded in such a grand enterprise since Caesar maneuvered his Gallic legions against the barbarians.

What it meant to Sherman's own troops is reflected in Edwin Weller's diary. Gone are the precise daily entries, penned at leisure while carrying out routine military chores. Now there isn't time. Instead he writes one long page to cover the final two months of 1864. He says:

"No diary kept from this date (Oct. 30) to Jany. 1865. However our army left Atlanta Ga. under command of Maj. Gen'l William T. Sherman Nov. 15th 1864 cutting loose from all communications and marching down through the country. Tearing up railroads, capturing horses and mules and taking all the provisions forage etc. needed to supply the army. (The city of Atlanta was destroyed before evacuating it.) [His insert]

"Our army met no opposition, except for a few guerrillas along our flanks, until we arrived near Savannah, Ga. We moved in four columns about ten miles distant from each other, foraging the country between the columns. Passed through all the principal towns in Southern Georgia, the following being the names of some of them. Decatur, Covington, Madison, Eatonton, Hillsboro, Milledgeville (capital of the state) Sandersville, Davisboro, Millen, Sylvania, Halagondale, Egypt, Marlow, Eden, and Bloomingdale.

"We came up to the enemy's works near Savannah on the tenth day December, formed our lines on the 14th. Gen'l Hazen's troops succeeded in capturing Fort McAlister which gave us communication with the gunboats off the entrance of the harbor to Savannah and communication with Washington, D.C. The remainder of the time up to the 23rd Dec. was occupied in skirmishing, taking advantage of the enemy at their weak points gaining advantageous positions and getting ready for a general assault on the works. The Rebs, learning of our plans, evacuated the City of Savannah on the night of the 23rd of December 1864.

"Crossing the Savannah River into South Carolina, we were to attack them at 5 a.m. the next morning but instead marched our army into the city and took possession. A delegation of the citizens of the city met our advance a little out of the city and surrendered it to our forces.

"We remained in the city 23 days and during that time made preparations for another forward movement against the enemy in South and North Carolina. During our stay in the city the city authorities and citizens conducted themselves with all due respect to our army, many of them seeming to be pleased with the change from Rebel to Federal forces and rule."

Then the diary resumes its regular brief entries, recording the winter rains and mud, the building of corduroy roads, the ceaseless foraging for food and horses as Sherman's army moved relentlessly northward.

During all the urgencies of combat he seems to have reached a new plateau in his young life. He was twenty-five and finally he had proposed to the girl he loved. From then his letters took on a new intimacy, not all roses, because he brooded about death and confessed to getting the blues sometimes, but now he expressed himself more openly. He could tell his hopes and fears to his beloved, and he poured them forth at every opportunity he found to write her.

Fragment, front page missing.
From *Savannah*, about 4 mi. N.
Mid *December* (?)

From Madison we marched to the capitol of the state, Millidgeville. Just before reaching the city Gen'l Slocum sent around an order detailing our Regt. and the 3rd Wisconsin to go forward and take possession of the city and capitol buildings. We found no enemy there, Gov. Brown having skedaddled with all his effects and the public papers and documents of the state. The flag of the 107th was the first to float to the breeze on the dome of the capitol of Georgia, but it was too badly riddled with bullets to stand the heavy winds of that day, so we were obliged to take it down and put up another.

We remained in Milledgeville nearly two days and were on duty in the city. All the rest of the Army were encamped about one mile out of the city. I, in company with several other officers, visited the state Insane Asylum located about one mile from town. It was a pitiful sight to see the inmates.

The professor of the Institute kindly showed us all through the different departments and gave us the history of many of the patients. There were between one and two hundred patients confined there, among them some fifty ladies. I saw some very fine looking young ladies there and particularly one, who formerely lived in Albany before the war. She had been deceived by a Rebel major who she was engaged to and it deranged her. But the professor informed me that she was convalescing. She seemed quite rational when we were there, and sat down at the piano in the ladies parlor and played and sang for us. She was a very fine performer on the piano. She took our names and we hers. The old professor was a staunch Union man.

From Milledgeville we marched to Sandersville and from thence to Louisville, and then to our present locality which is about 4 miles North of the city of Savannah. We destroyed all cotton along the line of our march, also took all the horses and mules we could find. I was relieved from the position of acting quartermaster of our Regt. a few days before we arrived in front of this city by the old Quartermaster, Lt. Howard. I turned over all the property of the Q. M. department to him and returned to the Regt. and was immediately placed in command of the Company. (Co. K.)

The second day after I returned to the Regt. we came up to a Rebel fort on the road, garrisoned, and they attempted to dispute our farther progress but we charged the fort and captured it with a part of its garrison and went on our way without meeting any opposition until we reached here where the Rebs are strongly fortified, and everything indicates another siege like that of Atlanta, but we shall eventually take the city.

A few days since, one division of the 15th Corps charged the Rebel fort McAlister and captured it, and its *whole* garrison and armiment, consisting of forty canon, and three hundred prisoners. The capture of that fort gave us communication with fleet and Gen'l Fosters forces in South Carolina. Yesterday Lt. Mr. Howard was ordered to report to Gen'l Easten for duty, consequently I am again acting Quartermaster of our Regt. and think it may be permanent.

Nett, I can hardly find words to express my thanks for the sweet assurance you manifest in your letters, of your affection for me. No one except a true, noble and patriotic young lady could express such sentiment and sometimes I have almost felt that I was unworthy to so noble and true a womans love, but I hope to merit the hand of such a woman at the expiration of my term of service.

Yes, Nett we will look only on the bright side of the future and hope for the realization of all our purest and brightest hopes for the future. And always when your thoughts wander to the Army and to one who is serving his country, rest assured that your love for him is reciprocated in its fullest extent and that his thoughts and affections are ever of you.

I am sorry to hear that you are afflicted with a sore hand and hope it may not prove at all serious for I hardly know what I should do if you were to loose the use of your hand so you could not write. It is indeed sad to hear of the death of Mrs. Campbell, she was truly a noble woman, and also the death of my highly esteemed friend Sylvester Mix. He was always one of my best friends. But such is life, short and of but few days on earth.

You speak of Fanny and Charley telling how much I think of a Miss Judson. Now Nettie, Charley knows better than that. He knows that I am not acquainted with the young lady and never spoke to her in my life. Neither did I write her. She is an old schoolmate of my sister Mary's and is much thought of by her. My sister sent me her photograph last summer as I was anxious to see what kind of a looking lady she was. My sister had so often spoken of her in her letters to me. I was to send the photograph back to sister but have never yet done so and presume I shall keep it now till I go home. . . .

But I must close as it is getting very late and I must retire. So good night and may God keep and guard you is ever the wish of your sincere and affectionate friend.

                                                              Ed

Write soon, I will write again in a few days.

Camp of 107th Regt N.Y.Vols
Savannah Ga Dec 24, 1864

Dear Nettie

We are at last in the
City of Savannah. it Surrendered
to us on the 21st Inst at 5 A.M.
The Enemy all skedaddled leaving
a large amount of Stores, Artillery
& Ammunition behind — all of which
fell into our possession. little did
I think when I wrote you, just a week
ago that we should have possession
of the city so Soon — Two days before
the Evacuation our Brigade was sent
across the River into South Carolina
to get possession of the main road
leading from Savannah to Charleston
but found quite a heavy force on the
opposite side to oppose them consequently we could not reach the road
in time to cut them off. This

From Camp of 107th Regt. N.Y. Vols
Savannah, Ga.
Dec. 24, 1864

Dear Nettie,

We are at last in the city of Savannah. It surrendered to us on the 21st Inst. at 5 A.M. The enemy all skedaddled leaving a *large* amount of stores, artillery, and ammunition behind — all of which fell into our possession. Little did I think when I wrote you *just* a week ago that we should have possession of the city so soon.

Two days before the evacuation, our Brigade was sent across the River into south Carolina to get possession of the main road leading from Savannah to Charleston but found quite heavy force on the opposite side to oppose them, consequently we could not reach the road in time to cut them off. This movement was undoubtedly the cause of their evacuating the place fearing that we would send across a heavy force and succeed in getting possession of the road and cut off their retreat.

We have certainly had far better success on this campaign than I anticipated when we left Atlanta. But it is all due to our gallant commander Gen'l Sherman who we consider invincible. *He never undertakes anything but that he brings it about.* I have not visited the city very much yet as we are encamped just in the suburbs of the city. I have been too busy with business in the Regt. I intend however to visit the city this P.M. as I have some business at the Division Headquarters. Those that have visited the city say that it is a fine place and plenty of pretty girls which you know is a great inducement to most men.

I received your very kind and very interesting letter of the 27th Nov. yesterday which makes me indebted to you one more letter, but in writing you I do not intend to wait for answers to each, but write every opportunity I have. You are so good to write me so often, and I hope you will continue to do so for there is no one whose letters are so gladly received as yours.

You did not say anything in your last letter about your lame hand. I hope it has got better and I came to the conclusion it had as you wrote me so soon after. In your letter of the 20th Nov. you said you had given Mr. V. a decided answer etc. He certainly took it less at heart than I should if I had received a like reply from you. But thank fortune it was not my doom; notwithstanding I have no doubt that Mr. Vail loved you, and well he might. As for me, I could not help but love you if I should try not to. Mr. V. was very kind to make you such a good promise as regards a present when you got married.

I have been thinking Nett — when, if ever, I should have married if I had not succeeded in a favorable reply from you, I think it would have been many years. I too, almost tremble when I think how near I came to losing you forever. How much more happy we now are, and soon hope to be, than we would have been if it had gone some other way. I was not aware before that Mr. Tracy took so much interest in my welfare, and I thank him from my inmost heart for the great kindness he has rendered me. I have always thought as much of Daniel Tracy as I could of a brother.

You now undoubtedly understand why I told Charley D. that you was not my style for a wife. I have been over a year constantly fooling that boy in regard to our affairs and I continue to do so. He and Fanny are too anxious to find out what we think of each other.

How strange it seems that we both should make up our minds to one thing on that evening I bid you good-bye, when I returned to the Regt. If I had known or suspicioned your sentiments toward me I should have told you my feelings without restraint but that time has gone and we will only look forward to brighter and happier days when we may be permitted to see each other daily and tell our feelings to each other, sharing each others joys and sorrows through life.

I have thought for a number of months that you thought a great deal of me, and for all you tried to conceal your feelings I readily saw through, but not until of late. And now Nettie, as we have become virtually engaged for life, we will make ourselves just as happy as possible in the thought that we shall soon be with each other and no fear of any more long separations. I have every confidence that you love me—and will again repeat what I have already said that there is no one in this wide world that I love so dearly as you.

Now that we have got in this city and good communications, I shall make a trial for a furlough. But I can hardly expect to get it as there are several officers in the Regt. who have never been home since they entered service, and I suppose they will have the first chance. But I want to get home very much as I should be so glad to see you. I am sure we could have a happy time while I remained.

But I shall be obliged to close as I have to go to the city in a few moments on business, in fact my horse is already at my quarters waiting for me. I shall write you again in a few days. I want you to write every week and I will do the same as I always love to write you and receive your good letters.

With much love, I am your affectionate Friend,

Ed

From Office of R.Q.M. 107th N.Y. Vols.
Savannah, Ga.
Dec. 30th 1864

Dear Nettie,

Having a few leisure moments before mounting my horse to appear on review this morning I improve them by writing you a few hasty lines that you may know that I am well and enjoying myself as well as possible. When you last wrote me you were feeling very lonely, and seemed to be in a very lonesome and meditative mood. You must not allow yourself to be prejudiced at all by such gloomy and unhappy thoughts, for they certainly can be no other but unhappy ones.

I dare not for a moment, if I would, look on the future of our lives, in any other light but that of happiness and contentment. Let us look forward and trust to Him who is all wise for the fulfillment of our every hope. If I were to allow myself to think for a moment that there was a doubt of my yet returning to my native state, no more to participate in the terrible strifes of war—and to claim one whom I have long loved as dearly as life, as my future partner in life, I should be unhappy indeed, but I look forward to a bright and happy future which you know I have long tried to picture for myself, and I have the greatest confidence that it will yet come. So be of good cheer—for dear Nettie, we shall yet meet and be happy I believe and trust.

Nett, if I had ever had any doubts, as to your devotion to me, your last letter would have dispelled them entirely, for it seemed to me that every word of that letter assured me that I need have no doubts on that point, if I ever had cherished such a one, which thank fortune I never have. Yes indeed, it is a happy thought to know that there is one though far away who loves, and I may say worships you.

How much I would give to see you. Over one long year has passed since that eventful night when I last bid you good bye. I can remember my thoughts and feelings on that occasion as well as if it was but last night. My heart seemed to come up in my throat and nearly choke me from uttering a word, but I braved it through. You little thought what the feelings of my inmost heart was that night, nor did I of yours.

Yes Nettie, we have been acquainted for about four years and during that time have associated together a great deal, always freely conversing on every subject, and quite often on that of matrimony and I do not know that we ever disagreed on any subject that we took up. As for myself I always considered you very consistent in your views on anything we conversed about.

Little did we think when giving each other our views on matrimony that we should hold the relative position, one to the other, that we now do, and as you say, it is very strange that we have never before revealed our friendship for each other. But it is probably for the best that we have not for now we fully know each other, and as you say we do not enter into this engagement blindly. And I ardently hope that ere another Thanksgiving shall appear our every wish shall be realized and our lives begun as one anew. May God speed the time for I long to see it.

I have been very busy indeed for the past two or three days in my office making out my monthly reports etc. Shall try and finish them this evening.

There is to be a review of our Corps today in the city by General Sherman. I had hoped to get rid of going, but as I am one of the Cols. staff, he expects me to be on hand. I expect we shall make a grand splurge on our parade through the city. The 20th Corps has the name of making the best appearance on all reviews and parades of any corps in this department. I wish you might be here to see it. You would undoubtedly pronounce it one of the finest sights you ever saw. Twenty thousand men all on a review would be a grand sight for those who never saw one. But we soldiers have become so accustomed to them what we think but little of them.

I was out to see the review of the 14th Corps a day or two ago. There was any quantity of ladies out to witness it. Savannah contains some twenty thousand inhabitants, and it can boast of lotts of pretty girls. I saw some splendid looking ladies out to the review the other day. I have not made the acquaintance of any of them yet as I have had to devote too much time to business to allow any time to be spent in that direction. I understand however from some of the officers who have made some acquaintances among them, that they show the greatest respect for the Yankees and that there is many 'Union Girls' among them. All those I have seen are very dressy indeed, always appear in the streets dressed in their fine silks and sattines. It is something quite new to see a southern lady dressed so extravegantly.

I believe I have not yet told you how I passed Thanksgiving and Christmas. Thanksgiving I was on the march all day and part of the night; did not get into camp till about one o'clock at night. So you see I knew but little of the day, hardly knew that it was Thanksgiving. Christmas I spent in our present camp getting my office ready for business — was quite forcably reminded of its being a holiday or some other extraordinary occasion, when I came to sit down to dinner; for I found the table bountifully supplied with broiled chicken, chicken pie, biscuit etc., gotten up in the most approved Army style. Aside from the dinner, the day

passed off like all others do in the Army — in the fulfillment
of our military duties. . . .

My office and the Colonels are together and we are trying
to enjoy ourselves as well as possible. Have a very good
house furnished in good army style consisting of one table,
one stand, washbowl and pitcher, two chairs and one camp
stool, and my office desk and table. There is a good fireplace
in our room. We live as happy as two old Bach's in our little
house. . . .

Did you attend the opening party at The Montour? How
did it pass off? I hope you had a fine time and enjoyed yourself well if you did go. How well I could enjoy a nice party
about now if I was where I could attend one. I think Nettie,
we would try triping the light fantastic toe together once
more, don't you think we would enjoy it?

This is probably the last letter I shall write you this year,
but a few more days and 1865 is upon us. Who knows what
another year will bring forth! May it bring peace, and honorable peace, and return the soldiers all to their homes, is
my fervent wish.

Yes, Nett the time is yet coming when we can bid each
other more affectionate good nights, than the mere writing
of them down, but a little over seven months and my time
expires. But I must close as it is time to go, the Regiment is
'falling in'. So good bye for the present and write soon.

Ever sincerely yours,
Ed

P.S. Nettie, will you please tell Leroy to send me one yard
of good heavy black rubber webb about an inch and a
quarter wide in his next letter or if he can not get it in that,

put it in a paper and send it, and I will ever be your loving friend.

Ed

From Office of A.R.Q.M., 107th N.Y.V.
Savannah, Ga.
January 7, 1865

Dear Nettie,

Nearly two weeks have elapsed since I last heard from you and this afternoon being alone in my office and nothing in particular to occupy my time, I concluded that the most plesant way to occupy the time would be to write you a few lines. I have made it a rule to write you every week since we arrived here where we could forward mail and you may be assured that I shall continue to do so unless prevented by unavoidable duties. It is no more than my duty to do this, as you are so kind to write me whenever your time will per mit.

Since I wrote you last our Regiment and Brigade have moved camp about a mile and a half toward the western part of the city and are located just in the suburbs of the city. Have a very nice camp. My office is located in a dwelling house and I again have the parlor of the house for my office room and a room just across the hall for storing my things in.

I am not as nicely situated as regards furniture as I was at Atlanta, but still I have enough to be quite comfortably situated. My furniture consists of a bedstead, bedding, etc. three chairs, one camp stool, one table and my office desk and table, also a wash bowl and pitcher. My room has a good fire place in it and just in front a nice portico which is very nice to display ones self just at eve, when the city people are out taking their evening rides and walks. There is no one who can enjoy such quarters so well as a soldier, who has just been on a hard campaign, yet my quarters would seem poor to people North I presume. That is the advantage of being a soldier, I shall be content probably with a limited amount of furniture etc. if I should be called upon to keep house.

I returned last evening from a two days foraging expedition. Went out in charge of a large train from here, about twenty miles. Did not have very good success as forage was quite scarce. I enjoyed the trip however. . . .

I brought in two families from the country and their effects besides ten or twelve negros. I was quite busy all this forenoon drawing and issueing clothing etc. to my Regiment. It is quite a nice job to issue clothing to a whole Regt. The quantity required for our Regiment would fill up a large size clothing store, so you can conclude what a task it is to draw and issue clothing for a Regt. every month.

There is a rumer in camp today that we shall probably march again in a few days, destination not known, probably Charleston. At least I hope it will be the next place to fall. There is nothing surer than that it will fall if Gen'l Sherman undertakes the job. He is a man that never fails to carry out what he undertakes. The citizens here are resuming business, and everything is going on regardless of the presence of our (Yankee) Army. I noticed in yesterdays paper that one of our Yankee officers has already united his destiny with one of the bells of Savannah. That, I think, must have been a case of "Love at first sight" don't you?

New years Day was quite dull here as we had just moved camp, and was hardly settled. I enjoyed a good dinner of chicken etc. gotten up by our celebrated colored cook who we (I mean our mess) think can not be excelled in the Army. And as a dessert we had some nice cherry wine which was sent me as a New Years present from Division Head Quarters. This is the first wine I have tasted of in nearly a year.

We have not received a mail in eight days; it seems almost a month. I am getting very anxious to hear from you. . . .

How I would like to be in H. I would invite a dear lady friend I know of there, to take a sleigh ride with me. She might refuse to ride out with a rough looking soldier boy but I think I would run the risk. I think I could enjoy a ride like those we had the winter before I came away, to Burdett, Millport, or Watkins, or any other place.

I wish there was some way to get a leave of absence. I want to go home very much indeed. How well I could enjoy a visit with you Nettie. I used to enjoy your sweet society very much before this war but how much better I could enjoy it now and how well you would enjoy it, think you? How often have I wished lately, sitting here in the office in my large arm chair, that my dearest friend, Nettie, might step in to my office and surprise me by her presence. And again I have wished I might make my appearance in H. and surprise you and all the rest of my friends. But such a thing can not be, so we shall have to be content yet a while. Every day is bringing our meeting closer. May God speed it, is ever my prayer.

But I must close, as I have to ride up to Brigade Head Quarters yet this P.M. on some business. Give my love to Mr. and Mrs. Tracy, Mrs. McGuire, Mrs. Woodhull and all others who may inquire. Write soon, and believe me ever your affectionate friend,

Ed.

Morning Jany 8th

I have just heard that our mail boat has arrived with a large mail for us but it has not yet been distributed to the Regiments. I am feeling quite out of sorts this morning with the tooth ache. My face is very badly swollen. I am going up to the surgeons office shortly to have some of them extracted,

Yours ever

Ed

From *Savannah, Ga.*
Sabbath Eve
Jany 15th 1865

Dear Nettie,

I have been looking anxiously for a letter from you for the past two weeks, and yet none has arrived from you. Yesterday there was a mail came in and I thought surely I should hear from you, but my desires were not gratified. And this evening while sitting in my office feeling lonely enough, my thoughts wandered to the quiet little village of H. and how I wished I might know how my dear friend Nettie is enjoying herself this (to me) lonely evening. Then I thought how dearly I should love to be seated as of old, with her, on that familiar sofa at her home, talking over our old scenes and social gatherings and the bright and happy future we have so often pictured for ourselves. How plesant it would be; yes indeed, many is the evening, when unincumbered with business affairs I sit in my office and think of you, and how dearly I love you and how comforting the thought that there is one, although far away, that loves you, and whom you love.

I am not very apt to get the blues, but quite often feel lonely and to drown these lonely spells I generally sit down and write to some of my friends. I wrote you just a week ago and this morning almost my first thought on arising was that I must write you today. At one time I was fearful I should be unable to do so, as I was detailed to go over in South Carolina with my train on some government business but I was very lucky and got my business done and returned to camp before night, and this eve I am fulfilling what I promised myself and you this morning. That is, to write you a letter.

There is no news here of consequence, only that we expect to start off on another campaign within the next two weeks. Gen'l Sherman is bound to keep at work at this rebellion and clean it out as soon as possible. He only rests his Army long enough at one time to get them well clothed up and recruited so as to be able to withstand the marches and fatigues consequent on campaigns like these of his getting up.

I have not received a letter since I came here, of later date that November 29th 1864 so you may easily imagin my anxiety to hear from you, and my relatives. Lt. Bryon was down to my office a day or two since and informed me of the fact that he has resigned and expects to go home as soon as his papers return from Corps Headquarters. I hear it rumered that Lt. Mitchell also thinks of resigning. Their reason I think for this is that there has lately been two men promoted to captains of their companies over them and men who were not in the service but pretend to have been in service once. I think such a thing a real outrage upon men who have served their country as long as they have. . . .

But I must close for this time hoping to hear from you very soon. I bid you an affectionate good night and plesant dreams. Ever your firm friend,

Ed

Direct via New York instead of Washington hereafter.

P.S. Monday morning Jany 16th

Dear Nett, I intended to have added another full sheet to this letter this morning but more clothing etc. has arrived for my regiment this morning, and I am compelled to issue it immediately as the news is that we have got to move. How true the rumer is I can not say. I will try however to write uou again just before we leave here if business is not too rushing.

No news of importance in the city this A.M. I have been trying for a day or two to get some photographs taken so as to send you one to let you see how your brave soldier boy is looking these days, but there has been such a rush at the gallery that I could not get the least chance, so I shall be compelled to abandon the project for the present. With love to you I bid you Adieu for this time.

Ed

Pulaski House
Savannah, Ga.
Jany 24th, 1865

Dear Nettie,

Your letters of Jany 6th and 9th came to hand today and I assure you they were very welcomely received. I had merely time to glance over their contense before taking a steamer from our camp some twenty five miles up the river, to this city. I arrived here at 6 P.M. came to this Hotel, took tea and on coming out from the dinning room found some officers (friends) awaiting me to accompany them to the theatre. I enjoyed the fun finely and have just returned and this moment finds me seated in my room writing my dearest friend on earth. Although it is eleven o'clock I was determined to write you before I slept this night. As I am here on Government business and probably shall be very busy all day tomorrow and therefore shall not have time to write letters.

Your last letters again doubly assure me of your pure affection for me. I wish I could find words to express my appreciation of your love. It seems we have both thought ourselves unworthy of each others but Nett I have come to the conclusion finally that such is the opinion of all those who fondly love each other. Therefore I think we must consider ourselves just fitted for the travelling of lifes rugged paths together and we shall yet be a happy couple. I have every confidence in you performing your part to that end and I think you have the same in me. But I must bid you an affectionate good-night as my light is failing and I will retire.

7 o'clock A.M. Jany 25th '65

Dear Nettie,

I wish you a good morning and will try and finish this letter before going down to my breakfast. Don't you think me quite an early riser to be up at 7 A.M. writing letters? It is surely quite early for me to get up when in camp, but there was so much noise in the hall this morning that I could not sleep. I am feeling finely this morning. I was just thinking how dearly I should love to be at Mr. D. Tracy's this morning and about this time be going down to bid you a good morning. I can well imagin how plesantly and with what smiles you would meet me. We should then be happy. I did not mean what I wrote you in regard to unhappy thoughts etc. as a chide. Not at all. Every person has unplesant and sad reminiscinces occasionally. I know I get the blues slightly occasionally and everything seems to go wrong with me, but I dispel such thoughts as soon as possible. . . .

Since I wrote you last my Division has moved up the river to a small place called Runysville in S.C. Steamers from here run up every day with supplies. I think we shall start on a campaign in a few days. I shall try and write you again before we move if I can send it out. But I must close as it is breakfast time and I have got a great deal of business to do today. Remember me to Mr. and Mrs. Tracy and all other friends in H.

Write soon and direct via New York City instead of Washington as letters come much quicker that way. With love to you my ever dear friend. I bid you Adieu,

Devotedly yours
Ed Weller

From *Robertsville, S.C.*
Febuary 1st, 1965

Dear Nettie,

Having an opportunity to send you a letter this morning I gladly improve it, yet I hardly know what I can muster up of interest to write you, but guess I can find something if it is no news.

I wrote you just a week ago while in the city of Savannah, which I presume you have received long ere this. I finished my business there the next day after writing you and the next day took the steamer for Peuryville. Was all day getting up the river. The boat got aground twice. The last time we were obliged to hail another steamer coming down the river to haul us off. Gen'l Williams and his staff were aboard and quite a number of other officers. The General is a very gay and lively fellow and we enjoyed the trip finely although it was very cold. We occupied the cabin, had a splendid breakfast and with-all a splendid time.

On arriving at Peurysville, I found that my Brigade had marched up the river some five miles that day and at first thought I should be obliged to walk that distance which would have been quite a jaunt for the night. But soon after leaving the boat I was very much pleased to see my colored boy come up with my horse. He took me through to the camp of the Regt. in a short time and over a road that I never had travelled before. I traced the wagon tracks and thus found my way through.

We have marched some three days since I returned and have encamped at this place for two or three days to wait for the remainder of the Corps to come up. The troops had quite a skirmish in occupying this little town. Wheelers whole Rebel Cavalry were here and attempted to dispute our right of possession but they were soon dispersed and the stars and stripes floating on the church spires.

You are indeed very good to write me so often and I can assure you they are sweet missives to me and dearly prized. I am glad that you prize my affection for you so highly for you certainly can not prize mine more than I do yours.

Your ride to Burdett and back to the party you speak of attending there must have brought back many happy recollections of our rides to and from that place. Yes indeed, what a vast change has come over that once united and happy circle of young people of Havana but few remain. You and I still remain, you in your native place and I in South Carolina as a soldier trying to defend the rights of my country. Indeed what a change. Surely who would have thought that three years would bring about such a change and now to think that we are engaged. How queer it seems and yet how grand to think of. It is indeed a happy thought to me.

I am considerably surprised to hear that Bryons girl gave him the slip as she did. And I agree with you that he is certainly fortunate in being thus rid of her and in possession of one no doubt who can more properly fill the station of wife.

I have entirely given up the idea of getting home this winter since this campaign has commenced and I think it very doubtful whether I get home at all before my time expires. But Nettie, you must keep up good spirits and look to the future for the realization of our dearest and brightest hopes. We shall yet meet and be happy. You speak of little Florence [Tracy]. She must be a cunning little creature by this time. She is just about the right age. I shall long remember the last night I was at your house, the night we took care of her after her father and mother had retired.

That was indeed a plesant night to me. And yet one of real sorrow when I was obliged to bid you adieu. . . .

I probably shall not have another chance to write you in two or three weeks for we are to start on a thorough campaign through this state in a few days and we shall not have any communications till we get some fifty miles from here to Broad River. But you must not fail to write as often as your time will permit and when ever there is the least chance of sending a letter to you I shall do so. Direct the same as I last directed You to and they will come all safe.

We are agin marching north and I hope it may be toward home. A little over six months more to march and fight but none of us know what may happen in that time. I hope for the best and trust that I shall live to see the glorious day of our reunion and the termination of my time of service. May God guard and protect both of us from all harm and afflictions is my fervent prayer.

This is a lovely day with us here—the sun is shining warm and clear, while you north are having cold and bleak winter weather with good sleighing to enjoy. But my dinner bell is ringing and I must go to dinner. Write soon.

From your ever true and sincere friend,
Ed Weller

The doomed Confederacy fought on, even though everyone knew the war was moving toward its end. After resting three weeks in Savannah, Sherman's army turned north and swept inexorably through South Carolina, which, as the cradle of Secession, had earned the North's bitterest enmity. The tragic price was now exacted in a campaign of fire and pillage. There are no other words for it.

Fighting was minimal. The only opposition to Sherman's progress came from small cavalry elements harassing the edges of his columns and attacking the small foraging parties sent out to scoop up what food and horses and other supplies were left in stricken South Carolina.

The Confederates still managed to take prisoners from the forage parties, but they could do no other damage. What combat the South could support was concentrated in Virginia, where Lee's armies were being slowly squeezed to death in the ruins of Richmond and Petersburg. There and in a few western sectors, the Confederacy fought on, though feebly.

Edwin Weller was himself a forager. He mentions flour, corn meal, sweet potatoes and ham as prizes that he particularly cherished—what a relief from the eternal hardtack. Larger prizes, such as the state capital at Columbia and the South's great arsenal at Fayetteville, are also taken, and their symbolism is not lost on the battle-weary soldier. Both prizes were destroyed and he notes that "the first ordinance of secession" was adopted in Columbia and that the Fayetteville Arsenal was chock-a-block with machinery looted by the South from the Harpers Ferry arsenal. Justice, he implies, has been done. And has been done with some compassion, at least in his view. Didn't Sherman's soldiers become more lenient in North Carolina, where they knew there were many Union sympathizers?

In North Carolina they saw the first friendly faces in many weeks. One brave girl even blew them a kiss. Certainly peace was in the air.

From Camp of 107th Regt. N.Y.V.
Fayettville, N.C.
March 12th, 1865

My Dear Nettie,

At last we have arrived at a place where we can again communicate with the outer world. Over six weeks have passed since we have had the privilage of sending out mail. We arrived at this point last night at 10 P.M. This city is located on the Cape Fear River some one hundred and ten miles above Willmington. It is one of the finest cities I have seen since leaving Savannah. We shall not remain here more than three or four days then push on to some other point. I think however we shall not go farther than Goldsboro which is located on the Neuse River, N.C. and there stop for a time and establish a base.

Probably ten days will finish this campaign — at least I hope so for we have been on the march constantly for nearly two months — have passed through some very fine country and some very poor. We marched through the heart of South Carolina and now are going through the heart of North Carolina. We have heard no news from the north since leaving Robertsville, when I last wrote you. I suppose you have heard nothing from us except through Rebel papers. We have been very successful thus far — have had no fighting with the enemy to speak of except occasional skirmishes with their cavalry.

We have had quite a number of men taken prisnors by the enemy since leaving Savannah. Some twenty from our Regt. among them was the 2nd Lt. of my company, Lt Whitehorns. We have also captured quite a large number of the Rebs; but I was fortunate this time and did not get captured as reported in H. on our other campaign to Savannah.

Nettie did you not begin to think you were not going to hear from me again while in the service? I began to be fearful I should not have an opportunity to write you again before my time expired but thank fortune my fears were unfounded.

Two transports came up the river this morning from Willmington with dispatches etc. and are going back this P.M. and take a mail. There is another steamer expected to arrive tomorrow. I really hope it may bring a mail for I am very anxious to hear from you and home. I was fortunate enough to receive a letter from you the very day we left Robertsville on this campaign.

My health has been first rate thus far on this campaign. We have lived on the fat of the land getting all our supplies by foraging on the country through which we are passing. Our principal food has been flour, corn meal, sweet potatoes, ham and various other articles in the way of dainties captured. We have had a long and tedious campaign so far but have enjoyed it quite well not withstanding the hardships.

Nettie, I have thought of you every day and how I longed to hear from you. It has seemed an age almost since I have received a word from you and I have no doubt the time has seemed equally long to you and you have been as much (if not more) anxious to hear from me.

But I hope there is a better day coming soon at least I hope and pray we may get where we can communicate with home and friends as often as possible for none of you at home know how anxious we soldiers are to hear from home and loved ones and the longer a person is in the service the more anxious he becomes. There is one consolation however—we have but five months more to serve before we can return to our homes and friends if spared. The time is growing short fast—every day lessens it.

The last letter I received from you was dated Jany 22nd but I did not have an opportunity to answer it. You seemed to think then that two weeks was a long time to be deprived of a letter from me but I fear this will seem almost an age. It has often been my wish that we were nearer each other where we could hear oftener from each other. But fate has decreed it otherwise.

You wrote that Havana was very gay this last winter. I am very glad to hear it and I have no doubt but that the splendid sleighing you had was well improved by all. I only wish I might have helped you enjoy some of it. It seems to me that the married people of H. are becoming very much demoralized getting so they dance and play cards. I should think Mr. Chester would disapprove of such things. Yet I suppose the customs in society have changed somewhat since this war began.

You spoke of meeting my brother at a party in Horse-Heads but I think you would change your opinion as regards the resemblance between us. I have changed very much since you saw me last. Become sunburned and so fleshy that I do not look at all natural.

I wish I might have been at that party; I should undoubtedly have enjoyed it hugely and then to have been in company with my dearest friend Nettie it would have indeed been grand. Your assurances of love for me were received with great pleasure and I assure you they are all fully appreciated and reciprocated by me. Every day strengthens my affections for you and I hope we may both be preserved to enjoy a happy and useful life together.

I shall hope to hear from you by our first mail. I will write you again when there is the least chance of sending out a letter. The conveniences for writing are quite limited with me at present and it has been so long since I have wrote a letter that I can not get a clear idea out of my head.

In short my ideas are slightly mixed and you must not condem this letter. I will try and do much better next time. I must close as the mail goes out in a very few moments.

Tell Daniel that Charley Cole was wounded and taken prisner by the enemy on the 8th Inst while out forageing. I send this word so he may inform his father, who is one of his customers. Remember me to Mr. and Mrs. Tracy and all others who may inquire. Write soon — Direct as before.

Affectionately Yours
Ed Weller

From Camp of 107th Regt. N.Y.V.
Near *Goldsboro, N.C.*
March 25th, 1865

Dear Nettie,

We are agin in camp and another long and dangerous campaign ended. We arrived here yesterday about noon and now occupy this city which gives us communication with Newbern by railroad and river and with Wilmington by railroad. The cars run through this morning for the first time, so we shall soon have supplies and clothing here for us.

But I assure you I am more anxious to get a mail than anything else at present. Just think of it Nettie, I have not heard from you in two months. It seems a very long time, and I presume it is some six weeks since you heard from me is it not? I wrote you a letter from Fayettville on the 12th Inst. but I hardly considered it a letter for it seemed impossible that day for me to get an idea on paper. I had been on the march nearly night and day for a week and the night before I wrote did not get into camp until about midnight, so I was in very dull condition to write letters.

Since we left Fayetteville we have had two quite hard fights but succeeded in driveing and whipping the enemy badly. In the last fight which was on the 19th and 20th Insts, we captured all the enemys hospitals with a large number of sick and wounded also several pieces of artillery and horses. I was fortunate enough to be out of these battles as I am still acting quartermaster of our Regiment. I think I wrote you of the capture of the 2nd Lieut. (Whitehorn) of my company, in my letter from Fayetteville. We have not heard anything from him yet.

We have received no mail since about the first of Febuary so you can realize how anxious I am to hear from home and friends. Yes Nettie, you can fully realize how anxious I am to hear from you. It seems an age to me and if I had not been on the march where there is something new to see and transpireing all the while I hardly know what I should have done. I thought of you every day and would wonder if you were well and enjoying yourself.

I hope such has been the case for I assure you it is a pleasure to me to know that you are enjoying life as well as circumstances will admit. We are expecting a mail tomorrow or next day. I shall look for several letters from you. We send out a mail this evening. All the boys of your acquaintance in the 141st and 107th are well I believe. . . .

I shall send a list of the casualties during the late campaign, in the 107th N.Y. Vols. to the Journal for publication in this mail for the information of the relatives of those who have been wounded and taken prisners. We expect to remain here in camp for some time, just how long I can not say but Gen'l Sherman sayes in his circular — long enough to get a good rest, clothed and fed up. I am thinking some of making an attempt to get a leave of absence to go to Nashville, Tenn. to get the baggage of our brigade stored there and bring it out here, but do not expect to succeed. Yet if I should, I shall try and get transportation by way of Elmira instead of Pittsburgh, Pa. In that case I could stop off a day or two at home and in H. . . .

It will seem very queer to become a citizen again after soldiering three years, but I think I can bear the change bravely. Nett, the old 3rd N.Y. Regiment is here with Gen'l Terrys forces. They are reinforcements for our Army. There is but fifty men left in their Regt. Their time is out in two months. I saw a young fellow by the name of Frank Smith who belongs to Co. K. He spoke of hearing some time since from your brother Charley at Harpers Ferry. He was then well. But I must close as the mail goes out in a few moments. Write soon as you get this. Give my kind regards to Mr. and Mrs. Tracy and family.

Truly and affectionately yours,
Ed Weller

From Camp of 107th N.Y. Vols.
Near *Goldsboro, N.C.*
March 26th, 1865

Dear Father,
Our campaign is closed and we are again in camp and in communication with America, home and friends. We arrived here day before yesterday in fine health and spirits after a long and dangerous campaign of fifty days, without a base or any communication with the outer world.

We marched through the very heart of the Confederacy going and doing as we pleased, subsisting entirely upon the country through which we passed. We found provisions in abundance and we all lived as well as we could wish on a campaign. Our course was through the central part of South and North Carolina hitting at all their wealthy and thriving cities and villages. In South Carolina we showed but little mercy to those hot headed and rebellious wretches but when in North Carolina we were a little more lenient knowing that there were many Union sympathizing people in that state.

We took and destroyed the capital of South Carolina, the place where the first ordinance of sucession was passed. (Columbia) Also took the State Arsenal of North Carolina, located at Fayettville. The machinery taken from the Harpers Ferry Arsenal at the commencement of the war, was carried there and put up and used for the manufactory of munitions of war for the Confederacy and was one of the largest in the South. We destroyed it and all its machinery. We found quite a large quantity of cannon and ammunition and small arms there all of which were destroyed.

Between Fayetteville, and this place we had two quite lively engagements with the enemy but came off victorious both times. They had concentrated armies from Charleston, Wilmington, and Hood's Army from Tennessee, against us but as usual Shermans name and presense was enough to put them to flight.

Our loss in our entire Army in the two engagements will probably reach one thousand in killed, wounded, and missing. We also lost about a thousand men taken prisner by the enemys Cavalry during the Campaign. They were men who were out foraging provisions. Lt. Whitehorn and two other men of my Regt. were captured while out foraging.

After our last fight the Rebs retreated during the night and as things show, in considerable haste.

The next morning at daylight Gen'l Killpatrick with his Cavalry, started in persuit coming up with their rear. He captured all their hospitals with their sick and wounded also sixty Battery horses and several peices of artillery. The Rebs loss in the engagements is estimated at five thousand. We took between one and two thousand prisners during our march.

Many of our prisners who were being moved from place made their escape from the enemy and came into our lines. Some of them had been prisners for nearly a year. They were happy fellows I assure you when they got within our lines.

Goldsboro is a very fine village of some four thousand inhabitants, nicely located two R.R.'s form a junction here, one from Newburn and the other from Wilmington. We also have communication by water up the Neuse river. So you can readily see that we have a good base, supplies are arriving fast. Today we received the first mail we have had since leaving Robertsville, the 1st of Febuary.

I was considerably disappointed however in not getting a letter from home. I shall expect in the next. I wrote Helen at Fayetteville, on the 12th Inst. My health has been first rate during the late campaign. I only hope it may continue good the remainder of my time—but I must close as it is bed time. Write soon. Give my love to all,

Your Affct. son
Edwin

From Office of Quartermaster 107th N.Y.V.
Near *Goldsboro, N.C*
March 30th, 1865

My Dear Nettie,

I was again the happy receipient of two of your very interesting letters—day before yesterday, one of Jany 29th
and the other of Feby 12th. Also received one yesterday of
Feby 23rd and Nett it would be entirely useless for me to
attempt to describe my happiness and the pleasure I experienced by their reciept and perusal. You can imagin something of my delight by your own experience when deprived
of letters from loved ones nearly 2 months.

I have perused and read and reread them many times
since their receipt and every time can discover some new assurance of your affection for me. Would that I had angels
wings how quickly would I transport myself to your side
and assure you in person that all the love you bear for me is
returned in the fullest extent. I certainly should be very
thankful that I have gained the affection of one so good and
true and that she is ere many months pass to become the
partner of my joys and sorrows. May the good being
preserve us both to see that happy event of our lives
transpire.

You seemed to feel somewhat dispirited when you wrote
me on the 29th of January and wished me with you. Yes,
Nettie, how gladly would I have exerted my every power to
dispelled your gloomy feelings if I could have been with
you, but keep up good courage, we shall yet have our antici-
pations all realized I trust. And Nett, whenever doubts arise
in your mind as to our ever seeing each other again, dispell
them with the thought that I should if at home be in danger
of diseases and accidents the same as I am here in the Army.

We are liable to be struck down by the monster death wherever we are, whether in the Army or in civilian life. You may be assured that I shall take the best care of myself possible, never failing to do my duty to my country and its causes.

I am anxious to see this war closed as I can be but never want to see it closed until an honorable peace and settlement can be brought about. Such is the wish of our whole Army.

I recieved a letter from Charley Duryea in the same mail with yours. He was enjoying himself hugely sleigh-riding etc. Said there was no news in H. Said not a word about Nett this time. I wonder what is the matter with him. Strange that he should say nothing about your affairs isn't it?

I think by your glowing discription of the parties and sleigh rides you have participated in that it has indeed been a gay winter north. In fact every one from whom I have heard confirms the same fact. I only wish I might have been with you to have enjoyed one, if no more, old fashioned sleigh ride, such as we used to have.

The people that were invited at your home that eve at 6 o'clock who expected that they were to witness a wedding must have felt a little disappointed — it was a good joke on them I should say. You say you wonder when people will give you up and cease their talk. I can tell you Nett, when you are married, and no sooner, don't you think so? And yet when you are married they will probably be very much surprised and disappointed.

You must be extremely careful Nettie and not work yourself sick for I should be very much grieved to hear of your illness. I am real sorry for you Nett, that you should be compelled to sleep alone such cold nights. It is really too bad and hope that you may not have occasion to make a similar complaint another winter. I agree with you, that people are sensible who marry before cold weather, but how is it in warm weather? But then I think that could easily be arranged, don't you?

Yes Nett, sixteen months has now elapsed since we have seen each other. A long time isn't it? It seems a very long time to me I assure you but as you say when we do meet the reunion will be the sweeter and I trust lasting. Just four months and a half have yet to pass before my time expires. Every day now shortens it some.

I should love to attend such a meeting as you speak of, where we could deliver our own sermons. I am of the opinion that we could edify as well as instruct each other.

But I must close as my horse is in waiting for me to go and transact some business connected with my office. Remember me to Louisa, Daniel and all others who may enquire. I shall make it a point to write you every week unless something unusual prevents me. Write soon. Ever remembering me as your best earthly friend for if this earth contains one I love dearly and devotedly it is your own sweet self.

With much love
          I am as ever your devotedly and affectionately,
                                        Ed Weller

From Office of Q.M. 107th N.Y. Vols.
Near *Goldsboro, N.C.*
April 2nd, 1865

My Dear Nettie,

Tis the Holy Sabbath day and quiet reigns supreme in the Camps of Shermans Grand Army for the first time in a long while. Today seems more like the Sabbaths used to at home, than any I have passed since leaving Atlanta. It is one of the finest days this year has been blessed with—warm, clear and healthy atmosphere.

I should have went to town to church this forenoon but for the reason that there is generally such a large crowd of soldiers going in, that it is almost impossible to gain entrance. So I concluded to stay at home and spend a part of the time in writing to you, my dearest friend on earth.

Your letter of the 23rd of Febuary was recieved several days since with the valentine enclosed for my perusal and I assure you I had a hearty laugh over it. It is indeed an amusing thing—the first and only one I have seen this year. Undoubtedly some one thought he or she was getting off a pretty good thing on you. I would advise whoever got it up to study the art of getting up poetry a little more, what do you think? Yet it is very good for what it is intended.

I wrote you four days ago, the 29th Ult., so you see I am a little more than fulfilling my promise to write you once a week. But I concluded it was no more than my duty and then there was a chance if I delayed writing today that I should not be able to write you before a week from today, as I expect to be very busy in my office all this week.

I am obliged to hurry up my business as there is a rumer that we are to commence another campaign on the 10th Inst. I am glad to hear that Louisa is getting much better.

You must have had your hands full while she was sick. No wonder your folks thought you sick and I have no doubt but that you would have been sick had it not been for your energetic disposition and strong will not to be sick. Daniel has cause to be thankful that you are there and render such valuable aids.

I used to notice your industrious qualities a great deal when I was at H. and always said when talking with young men of that town in regard to the industrious qualities of the young ladies of the place—that you done more work and was better acquainted with household work than any other young lady of H. And I think if there was more young ladies possessing your qualities, in the world than there is at the present day, there would be many more good wives and happy husbands than there is. What think you, Nett?

You speak of the Masonic Festival at H. I have heard through one or two others that it was a very fine affair. I am glad you enjoyed it well and should have liked very much to have been present and participated in the gayities of the occasion with you. I do not doubt but that you would have enjoyed it better as I am sure I should if in your company. It is sure, Nettie, that I do not have the privilage of any such enjoyments, yet I love to hear of your attending parties etc. and enjoying yourself as well as you can for what is life but to enjoy. . . .

I suppose the snow has all disappeared and you are now having nice spring weather are you not? I should think it would seem good to have spring come again. I have not seen any snow since a year ago this winter. It has seemed to me as if winter had been left out entirely, that the season took a gigantic leap from Fall to spring, forgetting to give winter her turn.

Charley Coryell was over and visited me night before

last. He is well and looks very much as of old. He expects to muster as 1st Lt. this week for three years longer. I am glad I am not in his boots, for I think when I have served my three years out, I have done my whole duty to my country and deserve a few months rest at least. Although today is Sunday, I feel just like having a good large train with some one, but suppose shall have to stand it without one. I will close as it is time for me to go out on a short ride with two other officers. My horse is being saddled for me now. Write soon, with much love to you, I am as ever yours Affectionately and devotedly,

Ed. Weller

9

As his twenty-sixth birthday nears, Edwin Weller is still a sword-carrying bit-player in the great final act of the Civil War, but his heart is elsewhere. Each rumor of surrender and each order winding down operations makes him certain the day of reunion with Nettie will be soon.

And though he turns detailed attention on his plans for their happy life together, he still keeps her informed on such diverse topics as his quartermasterly chores, the pretty girls in Raleigh, and his recurrent toothaches.

His confusion about the exact status of peace negotiations reflects widespread confusions of the time, a time that brought the terrible news of Lincoln's assassination and all its repercussions. Lincoln's death in fact is not mentioned in the letters, and in view of Weller's ardent campaigning for him this suggests that perhaps a letter or two, is missing.

From Office of R.Q.M. 107th N.Y.V.
Near *Goldsboro, N.C.*
April 7th, 1865

Dear Nettie,

I received your letter of March 26th just a few moments since and I assure you I was very glad to hear from you. I have been so very busy for the last week drawing and issueing clothing etc. to the Regiment and straightening up my accounts with the government that I have not had time to answer your letter of the 13th Ult. and now that I have got my business nearly finished up I will try and answer both of your letters in this one and hope to have another to answer before we leave here.

It is rumered that we start from here on another campaign, on the 10th Inst. but since the glorious news of the taking of Richmond by Gen'l Grants noble men I am of the opinion that we shall not move in a week or more from that time. The news of the capture of Richmond reached us officially yesterday morning and soon was known throughout our Army. It would have pleased you to have heard the shouts of hurrahs that went up for the noble Grant and his veteran Army. There was a general jubilee in every camp of our Army.

Yet I could not help but think of the many brave and noble fellows who must have fell victims to the Rebel bullet on that occasion and many who were severely wounded, suffering with shattered limbs and every other imaginable wounds. It is indeed sad to think of that so many lives are being sacraficed every day for such a detestable set of beings as these Rebs. But I am of the opinion that this rebellion is, as the Boys say, "about played out," and I hope before my time expires that my opinion may prove true.

News has just this moment reached us that the Rebel Gen'l Lee and nearly his whole Army are captured and in our hands. This is not official, however. . . .

You spoke of your sisters from U. Springs visiting you. I have come to the conclusion that you have a greater amount of patience than I have to be able to write a letter where so many children are making such a commotion. You must have a pretty clear head.

Then your sisters are anxious to know when they may come to your wedding are they? And don't know that we are engaged yet? Well, I must confess myself surprised. They might not be so well pleased over the matter if knew that the green and puny youth who used to clerk for Daniel, was the lucky one. Does Mrs. McGuire know of our engagement and what does she say on the subject? What do your father and mother think of it? I am of your opinion, that there will be quite a number of surprised individuals in that section especially among our old associates.

I received a letter from my sister Mary a few days ago and she asked me some pretty pointed questions as to when I was going to marry, and how soon after I get home etc., intimating that they suspicioned that I was deeply in love with some nice young lady, and I think they suspicioned about right. I wrote her in a day or two after and said she should know in due time who the fair one was. She seemed quite concerned about me, was afraid I would get to be an old Bach, as she has such a horror of old Bachlors.

By the way Nettie, how old do you suppose I will be day after tomorrow? The 9th Inst. I will let you guess, if you don't know. I think there is but little difference in our ages, however.

You undoubtedly remember my writing in the first letter I wrote you after we arrived here, that I was going to make an attempt to get a leave to Nashville after our stored baggage there and so get home for a day or two perhaps, but I could not get it. They sent a staff officer from HdQers Left Wing of our Army, so I shall give up all hopes of getting home before my time expires.

I hardly know what to say to you about getting tight and fainting away. I ought to give you a good scolding, hadn't I? But I will let it pass this time as I am not in a very good scolding mood today. But I think you ought to have made some calculations to fall into some nice fellows arms, why don't you? Just think of it if I had been there I should have made one grand plunge to have caught you. No wonder the company were frightened. I should have been if present on the occasion. I hardly think Tom and Jerry is good for you to take. . . .

The high water has made great ravages north, I see by the papers, I am glad to hear that Havana escaped so fortunately. Then Leroy has found out all about of engagement has he? Well, I can not say that I regret it at all. I expect to let all my folks know of it soon if they are not already advised on the subject.

They will all be pleased to learn of the thing, I am quite sure as they have often heard me speak of you when at home and could not help forming a very high opinion of you. Of course I used to then talk of the good and poor qualities of the different young ladies of H. but they always heard a good report for you That was before we were engaged but not before I looked forward hopefully for such an event.

I was just thinking of how long we have been engaged and if I remember right, it will be just about a year when my time expires in August next, will it not? It is getting so dark I can not see the lines hardly and my darky says come to supper. So I will drop pen etc. for a few moments.

Well Nettie, I have been to tea, and have been around to the Colonels Headquarters and picked my teeth so I guess I am ready to resume my pen again. Orders have just come to me to have my commissary Sergeant draw rations etc. and prepare for a campaign immediately. I have dispatched the young man accordingly. That means march sometime next week I should judge. The circular also says that the campaign is to last thirty days which means longer if necessary.

I had hoped to get a chance to rest a little before the campaign commenced but hardly think I shall get much. There is but little rest for Quartermasters when in camp—expecially when we do not remain long, as they have to see to the drawing of rations, clothing, forage etc. and issueing it to those entitled to said articles and make out returns of same to the government. I am responsible to the U. S. Government for one Army wagon, three horses and eight mules etc. beside all the clothing needed for the Regt. so you see I have no light responsibility on my hands. . . .

It really seems that I have been on the march almost constantly since we were engaged but Nettie, hope on hope ever. If I live I shall soon be free from this kind of life and we shall appreciate the happy meeting more fully, and I think possibly enjoy each others society quite as well as Fannie and Charley does. But I must close. I have written you a very long letter—if there is not much news or sense in

OVERLEAF   Lincoln Visits the Troops. *The President's towering figure became familiar to those within easy riding distance of Washington. Here he is posed with officers of a division encamped in northern Virginia.*

it. I will try and write you again before we move. Write soon. Give my kind regards to Mr. and Mrs. Tracy and all the rest of your sisters.

> Ever yours, affectionately and devotedly,
> Ed Weller

From Office of R.Q.M. 107th N.Y.V.
Near *Goldsboro, N.C.*
April 9th 1865

My Dear Nettie,

I wrote you day before yesterday but did not then know when we should start on the march. Today orders have come to march tomorrow morning at daylight. So I thought I must write you a letter informing you of the fact even if it be short.

This is my birthday, yet I could not rest. My time has been fully occupied during the day thus far, in getting everything in readiness for a move. Sundays seem to be as much a day of business here in the Army as others and I hope the time may soon come when we can be relieved of the unpleasant duty of working on Sunday. I was brought up to respect the Sabbath and rest from all labours but I find the Army customs of these days have no regard to a persons bringing up.

I should love dearly to be in H. today and have the pleasure of once more attending the Presbyterian Church and listening to one of Mr. Chesters good sermons. I presume I might also have the pleasure of your company to attend, if I behaved myself well. But such a thing is impossible and I will say no more about impossibilties.

Today is one of the finest days earth was ever blessed with — everything looks beautiful, fruit trees all in bloom and many of the trees clothed in their new suit of green. How beautiful is spring. I saw Phin Mitchell yesterday and had a good long chat with him. He gave me a full description of his visit home etc. and I should judge he had a very fine time. He spoke of you and said you were in fine spirits and looking fine as usual, which I was pleased to hear.

I have just received orders that the wagon train is not to move with the troops tomorrow morning, but will remain here for a day or two when they will be ordered up. So I shall have one or two days more rest than I supposed.

Well, Nettie, I shall be obliged to bid you an affectionate good bye for the present, as my horse is in waiting for me. I have some business to attend to that obliges me to see to immediately before the Regt. moves. Remember Nettie that I shall write you whenever an opportunity presents itself and I want you to write me often as your time will permit. May the good being guard and protect you is ever the wish of your

devoted friend,
Ed

P.S. I shall probably not have an opportunity to write you again for two or three weeks as we are going to close this rebellion on this campaign.

From Camp of 107th Regt. N.Y.V.
Raleigh, N.C.
April 15th, 1865

My Dear Nettie,

After a campaign of six days we have captured the capitol of North Carolina and compelled Gen'l Johnson with his Rebel Army to leave in great haste. And this moment a report has come in that Johnson with his whole Army has surrendered to Gen'l Howard commanding the Right Wing of our Army. God grant that it is true for if such be the case, this war is over.

I have always predicted that when this war did close, it would be suddenly and the surrender of Gen'l Lee of his whole forces and now that of Johnson (if true) will fulfill my prediction. Gov. Vance of this state had a consulation with Gen'l Sherman the day before we occupied this city and surrendered the state and all militia of the state under his control to the Government of the United States.

We arrived in this city yesterday and now have the railroad from Goldsboro to this place in operation—a distance of sixty miles. We found a large number of Union people here—and all seemed overjoyed to see us. It was said that quite a large number of the citizens were in favor of fireing a salute of a hundred guns for Gen'l Sherman on his arrival but for some reason, best known to themselves, did not do it. Deserters from the Rebel Army in large numbers were found secreted about the city awaiting our arrival. Large numbers of prisners have also been brought in beside a very large number of their sick and wounded left here in hospitals.

Raleigh is a very fine city about the size of Elmira but I

think rather nicer. I rode in company with several other officers through the city yesterday, saw lots of pretty girls, many of them displayed the stars and stripes and their white hankerchiefs as we passed by.

There is some of the finest flower and shrubery in this city that I ever saw. Most of the flower gardens were in full bloom which to us looked splendid. They were of the finest kind and superbly arranged. I think I should like to live here.

There was one little incident occured while we were riding through the city which was highly pleasing. We were riding through a splendid street on which most of the fine residences are located and passing an elegant mansion with a beautiful front yard and flower garden, but these were not the most attractive objects, for in the veranda stood two splendid looking young ladies. We of course let our horses walk along as slowly as possible so as to get a good look at them and when just in front of the veranda one of the fair damsels threw a kiss at us. Who it was intended for we did not know but we all returned the compliment. The fair ones seemed very much pleased over the affair and of course we were.

I do not know how long we shall remain here — probably no longer than today, if the report of Johnsons surrender should prove untrue, if it should be true we shall not move very soon. The mail goes out at 4 P.M. the first we have sent since leaving Goldsboro. You remember I wrote you the day before we left Goldsboro and then had orders not to move my train the next day, but I had no more than mailed that letter to you before orders came to move the next morning at 7 A.M. but did not move till 2 P.M.

I have been well and in fine spirits since I last wrote you.

Why should I not feel happy. A good prospect of the war closeing in a short time, a month or two at longest, then to get home to see my dear friends there. This with the assurance that there is one whom I love and who returns that affection, that I shall soon see and enjoy her sweet society, never more to be separated from her a long time—is enough to make any rational man happy—don't you think it is Nettie?

It has been raining nearly all day but has just cleared off and the sun has come out warm. We are camped in a grove on a beautiful hill near the state insane Asylum. I have not visited this institute yet but intend to today or tomorrow. There is a large number of patients there it is said, quite a number of ladies.

We have received no mail since leaving Goldsboro—I am in hopes, however we shall get one in a day or two for I am anxious to hear from you and home. I have reduced the number of my correspondents considerable since we were engaged for since that event I have cared but very little about corresponding with other young ladies. There is but little interest found in the correspondance with most ladies unless there is some motive in which the heart can enter.

I have got some pleasing incidents to tell you when I get home, about my correspondance with quite a number of young ladies who have ceased to be my correspondents within the past few months. What a huge chat we will have when I get home, just think of it—all that has transpired for nearly two years to relate. You will undoubtedly have a long list of transactions etc. to tell me and I know I shall have a long story to tell you of my experience in the sunny South.

But I must close as I have to write another letter to my Father before the mail goes out. Please excuse this scribbling as I have written this in great haste. Remember me to all my friends. With love to my Dear Nettie, and hopes for our union soon. I am as ever yours

Affectionately and Devotedly

Ed W.

Although Lincoln's death is not mentioned in these letters, Edwin's diary has something to say. Always laconic, recording mostly the weather and details of his military duties, the diary carries this unusual entry for April 17:

"In camp. Very pleasant and warm. Gen'l Sherman reported has gone to receive Gen'l Johnston. Sent out my wagon after forage in the country but did not succeed in getting any. Received the news of the assassination of President Lincoln. Went to bed with a hard toothache."

Next day he wrote:

"In camp. Warm and pleasant. The assassination of President Lincoln confirmed. Had one tooth extracted. Thunder showers during the evening. General gloom pervades throughout the whole army over the assassination of Lincoln. No news tonight."

Those bleak words, read a century later, still convey the tension of a terrible moment in history. Thunder showers, toothache, assassination and general gloom—perhaps the feelings were too deep to be expressed in letters.

In any event, the army soon moved on slowly northward and the flow of letters was uninterrupted.

From Office of Regt. Q.M. 107th N.Y.V.
Raleigh, N.C.
April 21st, 1865

My Dear Nettie,

Your very kind letter of the 9th Inst. was welcomed with delight today and if it has been read once it has many times. I also received one from each friend Duryea and Lt Byron in the same mail. And that picture of the "Mutual Tight Hold Association" Charley sent me, was decidedly the gayest thing I ever saw. If you could only have witnessed the reception of that article as I was lying on my bunk, you would have thought me going into spasms. I have not had such a hearty laugh in a long long time as I had over that likeness.

It is really too bad for Charley to send such a tantalizing picture to a poor soldier boy who is away down in Dixie and of course can not realize anything pertaining to the aforesaid association. Yet I must confess, I sympathise with Charley deeply and I should with any young man who should happen to be thus situated.

I should consider myself lost entirely if situated as he is represented in the likeness. You know I am not used to such usage, never indulged in anything of the kind. Oh, no, certainly not. Had you learned Nett, that I have given up all such practices? That is until I get home. Well it is so. I expect when I get home I shall have forgotten all about such things but I shall have some good instructors I presume to re-*lie* on. What think you.

It hardly seems possible that nearly two years have elapsed since I saw you. Yet the time seems long. But Nettie the glorious news from Richmond and other places and now the final closeing is being consummated here by Gen'l

Sherman and Gen'l Johnson, Jeff Davis and other high officials of the so called Rebel government. They have accepted Gen'l Shermans terms, which is the surrender of the whole Southern states, and the Rebel Army to the government of the United States and peace to be proclaimed through out the states.

The proceedings have been forwarded to Washington for ratification and when ratified will bring peace and lasting peace to our glorious country. How many happy hearts such an event will make; may God hasten the day.

Gen'l Sherman announced yesterday in an official order that hostilities has ceased and that he hoped and believed that he would soon be able to convey us all to our homes. He also ordered the Troops to go into permanent camps near the city and select good grounds. Does this not look like the end of the war Nettie?

I am now making calculations to be home about the 1st of July so that will make me but little over two months yet to stay in this southern land. Then I shall see you once more. Since this war has looked so near a close I have been so anxious to get home.

I have been afflicted for three or four days past with a very hard tooth ache and to day getting out of all sorts, I determined to have them extracted. So over to the Surgeons office I went and had two out. I am now feeling like myself again.

I think Charley extremely fortunate in being allowed so lengthy a furlough to visit his friends in the country. He seems to be having a lovely time with his Fanny. She is a splendid looking lady. Yet for all that, give me my true and lovely Nettie. Without any joking or flattery, Nett, I think I never saw any one look so lovely as you do in that likeness that Charley sent me. I could not help but look at your picture with pride and pleasure and my only hope and prayer is that I may live to meet you again. There is not a day passes but that I think of you and the bright and happy future before us. . . .

I am sincerely glad to hear that the knowledge of my affection for you should aid you to while away the lonely hours and I trust that when I return, to remain in the future, that my society will dispel all gloom and sorrows. Such, I am confident, will be the effect of your sweet society upon me. I tell you Nettie, we shall yet be very happy. I feel that it is to be so. . . .

We expect to move camp this afternoon but a short distance from where we are now located. I wrote Daniel day before yesterday. I also wrote you by the first mail that went out after the occupation of this place. I see you wrote me the same day I last wrote you before leaving Goldsboro, the 9th Inst which was my birthday. But I must close as I have some other writing to do today appertaining to my office. Write as often as you can, and I will do likewise.

Devotedly yours,
Edwin Weller

Sunday morning April 21st

I failed to get my letter written in time to go out in the mail yesterday as the mail boy neglected to call for it, but I will add more to it this morning and forward it today. I rode down to the city last evening in company with several other officers and called on some officers of our acquaintance on duty there. Had a very pleasant time. Was treated to a splendid supper which is considered by us who have been constantly on campaigns as a great rarity. I assure you we did justice to the occasion.

It is raining very hard this morning and I have hardly been out of my tent yet. Tell Daniel that I received the hat he sent me by express last evening in good order. It suits me very well indeed.

You are very right Nettie, we could care but little as to the state of the weather out doors if we were seated in your snug little parlor as of old, conversing freely on the subjects nearest our hearts and which we look forward to with anxiety. That day is coming and I trust not far distant. The time is flying away rapidly, four weeks, I think, will see me a citizen again and in the sweet enjoyment of the society of near and dear friends. . . .

I was thinking, but yesterday, what a lonely life mine would have been since I returned to the Army from home had it not been for the sweet misives I have received from you, always full of hope and encouragement. I am quite confident that you can not fully realize what a source of pleasure and hope they have been to me. . . .

LeRoy writes me that Duryea expects to get his discharge soon probably before our Regiment returns home. He also is strongly of the opinion that he contemplates matrimony sometime during the summer. How strange it is that so many emigrate to that state, but not all alike — happy in that state. many a life is made wretched by the change, and on the other hand many are made supremely happy. How many different features of life exist in our land. Some happy, others miserable and wretched.

But my opinion is that most of the misery and wretchedness existing in our country is brought on those who lead such a life, by themselves. There is no need of a man and wife living unhappy if their union is prompted by genuine affection. I think you and I were always of one opinion in regard to that point. Never to marry one whom we did not sincerely love, that has always been my motto, and I am now reaping the pleasure of such a resolution and hope ere long to have my happiness more complete.

My opinions of love, I recollect, used to be very limited until I become fully acquainted with you; then it sprung forth and has been growing brighter and brighter every day since and now my whole heart is wrapped up in the strong attachment and love I have for you, my dearest of friends. May bright angels ever watch over and guard you, is the prayer of your

Affianced
Ed

A false alarm of renewed fighting, then real peace. The great army trudges slowly northward. Edwin Weller and his foragers are riding a parallel route, buying grain, dining with plantation owners, and finally visiting Richmond in ruins. And last of all the historic Grand Review in Washington.

From in the Field
Jones Cross Roads, North Carolina
April 26, 1865

My Dear Nettie,

Having an opportunity to send a letter to Raleigh I scribble you a few hastily written lines. When I last wrote you the general impression in our Army was that our fighting was over and that peace would soon be proclaimed and I must confess that I had the greatest confidence that the negotiations between Gen'l Sherman and Gen'l Johnson would result in his (Johnstons) surrender and thus the war at an end. But Gen'l Sherman did not propose to let all the leaders of this Rebel clan off so easy and give them full pardon after being the cause of the sacrafice of so many noble lives and so much misery in our country.* It was indeed a wise decision and I sincerely hope that the leaders of this Rebellion may be caught and rightly dealt with.

We left Raleigh yesterday morning on short notice arriving here at 3 P.M. yesterday. We shall probably remain here all day but as soon as the whole Army gets up, we shall move on the enemy. It is the intention of Sherman to compell Johnston to surrender his whole Army or destroy his Army for him. The fate of the so called Southern Confederacy is doomed.

The war can not last but a month or two at most and I sincerely hope and believe that ere my time expires this

---

* *Weller's information was faulty. What had happened was that Sherman, the war's greatest villain in Southern eyes, had offered Johnston peace terms much softer than Grant had given Lee at Appomattox. When Washington, still chaotic after Lincoln's death a few days earlier, saw Sherman's terms, the government refused to approve and peace had to be renegotiated, this time making sure that only military matters were covered and that political decisions were left to civilian leaders.*

fratricidal war will have been brought to a close. What rejoicing there will be in the Army and among the friends of the soldiers. I long for that happy day to arrive when I may once more return to my home and dear friends to again enjoy their sweet society and become a quiet and peacable citizen of the North.

We are having beautiful weather here now and everything is favorable for a campaign. I enjoy marching through this country at this time of the year much more than at other times of the year for now the trees are all leaved out, and flower gardens in full bloom. Strawberries and garden sauce begin to appear and all nature looks beautiful.

Yet I would exchange all these pleasant scenes gladly for a return to my friends North. How much more I could enjoy a visit home. But never mind, Nettie, I shall soon be with you if fortune favors me.

I am making some very brilliant plans for the future when I get home. I am going to devote about two months to visiting my friends and have a general resting out from my Army life. Then I am going to settle down in business and become a steady man.

Don't you think such a course advisable for so wild and unsteady youth as me? You don't know what a wild fellow I have become since I last saw you. But the mail boy has come for this letter and I must close. I do not know what I shall have another opportunity to write you but will do so the first I have. Remember me to all my friends in H., especially Mr. And Mrs. Tracy.

With much love I am devotedly yours

Ed

From Office of Regt. Q.M. 107th N.Y.V.
Raleigh, N.C.
April 29th, 1865
My Dear Nettie,

We are back to the city of Raleigh again. I wrote you a few days ago at Jones Cross Roads some fifteen miles from here. The prospects then were that we should be obliged to fight Gen'l Johnstons Rebel Army to compell them to surrender but the very day I wrote you Johnston surrendered his whole Army to Gen'l Sherman consisting of all the remaining Rebel Army except that in Texas and Arkansas which he does not have control of, I believe.

Johnston saw that Gen'l Sherman had made such a disposition of his troops that he would eventually be compelled to surrender his army. He undoubtedly thought it much better to surrender the remnants of it to Gen'l S. I think his doing so shows that he thought descretion the better part of valor and was a wise move on his part.

The war has now closed without doubt and we may soon expect peace with all its blessings to be proclaimed throughout the North and South. "All hail the happy day."

I received your very kind letter of the 14th Inst day before yesterday and the many assurances of your affection for me it contained was received with pride and admiration. Such assureances go very far toward smoothing my rough life as a soldier in the field. God knows I hope I am worthy of such a pure and unsullied love as yours for I try to be. . . .

We start for the North tomorrow morning to what point I have not learned positively but conclude it is Washington as our Surgeons have orders to convey their sick to Washington and there report to their respective commands. We are to go via Richmond so we shall have the pleasure of seeing the Rebel capitol.

I am of the opinion that we shall not get mustered out till about the 1st of July next, but I shall be quite well satisfied to get out then, not having any more fighting to do. I shall send Daniel yesterdays and todays Daily Raleigh papers which contain all the news of Johnstons surrender and our march for the North.

There seems to be something the matter or else you have been having a discussion with someone on matters and things as you have been vexed in some way so as to affect your happiness, I think by what you say in regard to the other letter you wrote. I did not see anything wrong about it, at least I enjoyed reading it very much. You seem a little doubtful as to my anxiety to hear from you or rather that I can not think as much of your letters as you do of mine as they are not so interesting.

Let me inform you that you labour under quite a mistake for I can assure you that I look for the arrival of your letters with as much interest as you possibly can mine and if you could take a shy peep into my office when perusing them you would readily see an interest displayed in the perusal of them, that is shown in no letters, except when true affection abides for its fair writer.

I should indeed like to have been a mouse in one corner somewhere so I could have heard the many bets made by Mrs. McG. as regards your marriage. I have no doubt but they were interesting in the extreme. I am a little anxious to know what the bet was but suppose I shall have to be content until some future day. You wish to know my opinion as to whether she will lose or not. I rather think she will lose if I can have my wish and am permitted to return home safe and in good health.

I believe we have never said anything to each other in

regard to the time we should be married but I will tell you what my idea is as I have been thinking some on the subject of late. I wish to get nicely located in business of some kind before that event occurs and be enabled to support a wife as she should be. I have always had my own opinion as to how a young man should be situated when commencing life and I still maintain the same opinion, that it is every mans duty when he marries to be in some business by which he can gain a good livelihood for himself and wife.

I intend going into business as soon after I return home as circumstances will admit. That is as soon as I get well rested out and if I succeed in establishing myself in business I should like to be married sometime in November next. Of course I shall be governed by your wishes in regard to the matter.

You ask if I am not fearful that you will become tired of work and discard it altogether. Not in the least Nettie. I know your disposition in that direction too well but I do not intend you shall ever work so hard as you have during a few years past. You must not be too well assured that you are to have the best husband in the world for I do not wish you to be decieved in me. Yet I shall try to be the best I can and if I should fall in any point it will not be intentionally but through ignorance. I am happy to know that you place such implicit confidence in me. We shall indeed both have something to work for and that is each others happiness and comforts. I am fully confident that you will do every thing that a wife can do for a husband and I am also confident that I shall have the best wife I could possibly wish for. We will both work for each others happiness. Please accept my thanks for your Photograph. It is very good indeed. . . .

It will not be long now Nettie, before we shall see each

other again I hope. Probably two months at fartherest. We
can then communicate our thoughts and wishes more freely
and direct to each other and not be compelled to write
down on paper our desires and hopes. I look anxiously
forward to that happy day. But I must close as I have many
preparations to make for moving tomorrow.

You may not hear from me till we reach Richmond but
be assured I shall write you whenever opportunity offers.
Write me as often as possible and I will receive them at
Richmond or Washington. Give my kind regards to Mr. and
Mrs. Tracy, Mrs. McGuire, Mrs. Woodhull and Sarah
Woodhull and all other friends.

With much love I am devotedly your
Ed

From Bivouac of 107th Regt. N.Y.V.
8 miles South West of *Richmond*
May 9th, 1865

My Dear Nettie,
We have at last arrived near the fallen city of Richmond.
We arrived here yesterday afternoon about 3 o'clock. Our
mail goes to Richmond this morning at 8 A.M. and I thought
I must write you a few lines at least. I am well with the exception of a slight tooth ache, and have enjoyed our march
from Raleigh so far very much. We have passed through
some very fine country and new to us. I have been quite
busy during the march foraging grain etc. for our Brigade,

having been detailed for that purpose. I had a Leiut. and six men to assist me. We generally travelled on a separate road from that traveled on by the main colum and whenever we found grain that we could buy — sent one of my men to the colum and bring up wagons to load it in.

I found it a very pleasant way of traveling as we were free from dust and the crowds, also could take our own time. Stop at all the plantations and see the young ladies, which we found in abundance. We of course took our meals with the planters whenever we happened to stop at meal time, consequently lived good for soldiers. We generally, of course, hit upon a plantation where there were some good looking damsels, for our dinner. We had a great deal of sport I assure you but we have now to go into a section where foraging is out of the question, it being too near Richmond.

We expect to cross the James River above Richmond this P.M. or tommorrow. I am fearful we shall not get a sight at the city — yet I intend to visit it if we go within five miles. We expect to get to Washington in about a week, where we shall remain two or three weeks and then go to Elmira and be mustered out.

I am getting quite anxious that we should hurry things for the sooner we get through to W. the sooner we shall be mustered out and I shall get home and see you, my dearest earthly friend once more. What a happy day that will be. I

OVERLEAF   Welcome to Washington. *The Grand Review lasted for two days, May 24–25, 1865, bringing the vast armies of General William T. Sherman and General U. S. Grant down Pennsylvania Avenue to be reviewed by their new commander-in-chief, President Andrew Johnson. The parade was of a magnitude never matched in American history.*

have thought of you many times during our march and in fact you are hardly absent from my thoughts a moment. Love is indeed a strong tie and a sacred one.

I am in hopes our mail boy will bring a mail back with him as I am very anxious to hear from you. We have received no mail since leaving Raleigh. But I shall be obliged to close as the mail goes out in a very few moments. Write often and direct to Washington D.C. Remember me to all.

Ever your devoted
Ed

P.S. Enclosed I send you a letter from a Rebel girl of Nashville, Tenn, which I consider decidedly the best thing I have seen in a long time. It shows how sudden they are apt to change their minds and their preferance for the Yankee officers and soldiers to their own. Please preserve it.

Ed

From Office of Regt. Q.M. 107th N.Y.V.
Near *Alexandria, Va.*
May 20th, 1865

My Dear Nettie,

I have just this moment received a letter from you dated April 20th the first I have received since leaving Raleigh and I assure you it was gladly hailed. I have not had time to peruse it but once through — being obliged to write immediately if I sent a letter in todays mail.

I usually read your letters over many times as I love to peruse them so dearly. You write such splendid letters, full of assurance of your devotion and affection for me.

Our Army arrived here yesterday at 4 P.M. and went into camp. We are stationed about two miles out from Alexandria. We are to have a grand review of the 24th Inst. of Shermans Army and one of the Army of the Potomac on the 23rd. It is thought that all the troops whose times will expire within the next six months will be mustered out of service immediately. I hope such may be the case as now that the War has closed, I am more anxious to get home. There is but little excitement in the Army now.

We had a very plesant trip through from Raleigh, were blessed with very fine weather and good roads, had but one rainey day during the whole march. I wrote you at Richmond or rather near there.

We were reviewed when passing through the city. I rode all through the city with several other officers. Saw Gen'l Lee's house and Jeff Davis mansion, also Castle Thunder and Libby Prison and many other celebrated mansions. Richmond was once been a splendid city and some parts of it is still but the business portion is quite badly dilapidated and shows the effects of war very plainly.

I received a letter from brother Leroy today also one from sister Mary. Leroy speaks of the conversation he had with Daniel and how he found out you and I were engaged. He seems very much pleased over it and congratulates me on my good luck in getting so splendid a partner for life. He says he only hopes he may get as good a one if he should ever marry. My folks have been informed of the fact, I suppose by him and they are highly pleased with the arrangement.

I am now of the opinion that I shall get home about the middle of next month. I shall be very busy settling up my business with the Government while here but do not intend to commence till after the Review.

You found out my age and whole history without much difficulty, I should judge. What do you think of it? I thought that you were about 25 years of age and about one year younger than myself. Surely the differance is slight much better as you say, then 25 years difference. I approve of your course in not telling your friends of the engagement between us. It will undoubtedly spread enough after it is held as no secret from anyone.

I have been interrupted so often since commencing this letter that I hardly know what I have written. Nearly every officer has been in for something or to ask some trivial question. But I must close before the mail goes out and leaves this behind. Give my love to all. Write soon.

With much Love, I am as ever,
Yours devotedly
Ed

From Office of Regt. Quartermaster 107th N.Y.V.
May 27th, 1865
Near Bladensburgh, Md.

My Dear Nettie,

I have been the happy recipient of two letters from you within the past week and should have written you again before this time had it not been for the pressure of business connect with my office. I have been constainly on the go or at work at my desk for the past week and this evening I determined to write you a few lines at least, although I should not have attempted to write any one beside you. I deem it a duty as well as a great privilage to write you my dearest earthly friend. I am hoping soon to see you and I trust that desire will be granted me ere many days of nothing unusual transpires.

All that now hinders us from going home is the getting of our papers ready to be mustered out and they are being made out as fast as possible. I think we shall start for home the last of next week or the first of the week after.

You have undoubtedly read the account of our Grand Review on the 24th Inst in the newspaper, therefore it is useless for me to repeat it. Suffice, that we had one of the grandest military displays ever witnessed in this country. I took part in the performances and I never expect to take part in or witness so grand a sight and display again during my life.

It was a very large number of citizens from the North and West to witness the Review. All seemed greatly disapointed in Gen'l Shermans Army, it did so much better than they expected. We are even credited with doing better than the Army of the Potomac. I only wish you might have been witness to the grand affair. . . .

Yes Nettie, the dark clouds have nearly all disappeared and soon we shall meet again. I trust never to be parted so long again. We can then take a quiet stroll together and enjoy each others society without fear of separation. I look forward to those days with much pleasure and I sincerely trust that no clouds may arrise to darken our pleasures in the future. Yes Nettie, you will have to be very careful or you will frighten me at our first meeting. You must bear in

mind what a modest youth I am and how easily I am em-
barrassed for if you don't I may lose my composure and
dignity and make a bad display of myself. Now do try and
be cool and composed for my sake, won't you?

I am thinking I shall accept you as my instructor to teach
me how these affectionate demonstrations to ward the fair
sex should be made. I am quite confident that I could learn
rapidly under your untiring instructions. I suppose you will
not object to undertaking the task, will you? You may consider yourself as engaged for the job. It gives me great pleasure to know that you have become so light hearted and
happy over the prospects of soon seeing me. I shall surely
try to merit such high esteem. . . .

I am feeling in good trim to have a train with some one
tonight but will wait patiently till I get home. It is about
eleven o'clock and time to retire as I am quite tired tonight
with my days labour. I do not think it advisable for you to
write me again after the reception of this letter as I should
probably never receive it.

We shall start for Elmira as soon as our papers are
finished which will be but a few days. Remember me to all
my friends. With a God bless you and an affectionate good
night, I am ever yours

With much love,
Ed. W.

10

No more letters were necessary.

By June 7 the regiment had reached Elmira, where bands and flowers greeted the returning soldiers. Quickly the paperwork was completed and they were mustered out just two months short of their three-year enlistments. Then on the evening of June 9 Company H achieved the one thing in life all its members wanted—to get home to Havana.

And Havana lived up to the grand occasion. The boys in their well-worn blue marched around the tiny village square, their path strewn with flowers and the Havana brass band pouring its heart out.

The march ended at the new Montour House, where a chorus of little girls standing on the balcony sang "The Red, White and Blue."

Indoors, a lavish dinner waited on tables banked with roses, lilac, lilies, and all the other June blossoms that willing village gardens could yield. The speeches went on and on, but probably no one minded.

Five months later, just as he had planned it, Edwin Weller and Antionette Watkins were married, on November 15, 1865.

Whether or not they lived happily ever after is hard to say now, more than a century later, but the evidence, what there is of it, points that way.

Edwin put aside his well-worn uniform and went back to work in Daniel Tracy's dry-goods store. He was twenty-six, and his status there was somewhat improved: he and Daniel were married to sisters. And in time he bought out Daniel Tracy's interest and slowly became one of the village's leading merchants.

Nettie, everyone agreed, was a good housekeeper. As the youngest of six girls she had had ample experience helping out when her older sisters married and started families. In the next fifteen years, Nettie bore six children, four girls and two boys.

Their memories of childhood were more than ordinarily radiant. In later years they reminisced about constant coasting parties in the long York State winters, about glorious family dinners, about attending Cook Academy, a private local secondary school, and about gathering bucketsful of wild daisies to decorate the Weller house on festive occasions.

The outdoors seems to have been an important part of Havana life. After all, the woods and hills began right across the street from the Weller house. And Montour Falls, an impressive natural phenomenon, was only a block away.

That deep attachment to nature lasted long after childhood and they had scattered to make lives of their own, some in distant places. My own mother, the third daughter, lived in Illinois with her newspaper-editor husband. For her, the arrival of spring, on her own birthday, March 21, was not marked by the arrival of daffodils or the first robin, but by the arrival of a big package from Havana, now called Montour Falls. Inside, packed in damp natural moss, was always a huge bouquet of delicate pink trailing arbutus, a flower that heralded spring in New York but was unknown to Illinois. The ties were very strong.

His children said that Edwin Weller seldom talked about the

Civil War, but its importance to him was never in doubt. Whenever the 107th New York Volunteers had a reunion, most often in Elmira, he was there. One year a trainload of veterans went back to Antietam. Twenty years had elapsed since that night they had bivouacked in a dew-wet clover field, awaiting their battle baptism next day. They found the scene remarkably unchanged. Edwin wandered with his comrades across the fields and through the woods, even finding battle debris — rusting canteens, bullets, buttons — still lying where it had fallen that fateful day.

Those reunions were dear to him, and he left scrapbooks crowded with clippings that record the speeches, picnics and parades that were a feature of the last decades of ninteenth-century American life.

After his death in 1908, Nettie lived on with an unmarried daughter in the roomy old house filled with the possessions of a lifetime. I remember her, on summer visits, as a model grandmother who kept a well-filled stone cookie jar by the cool spring in her cellar. Tart-tongued and spry, she made mild mischief among her descendants and laughed gaily when people seemed to take her talk too seriously.

At long last, in her ninetieth year, Nettie began to fail. My mother and I journeyed East to find her bedridden but still sprightly. When I approached her bedside, she looked up at me for a long moment, then with a dazzling smile threw back the bedcovers and said, "Good morning, Mr. Muller. Would you like to climb in?"

One of her more churchly daughters, standing nearby, gasped saying, "Mother, that is not Mr. Muller. That is your grandson."

Then, withdrawing to a corner of the room, she added in shocked tones, "Louise, did you hear what Mother said? Do you suppose. . .?

Later, I asked, "Who was Mr. Muller? Someone she used to know?"

"The Methodist minister long ago," my mother replied.

Nettie's funeral, on a suddenly chilly April day, was an Anglican service in her own front parlor, the words barely audible to her family clustered on folding chairs in the upstairs hall according to local custom.

In the ancient bright green cemetery high above Montour Falls, she was buried next to Edwin Weller, who had fought at Antietam and Gettysburg. On the other side stood a monument to her grandfather which records the fact that he spent a winter once with George Washington at Valley Forge.

Later, back in Nettie's house, the family gathered for the ritual tea and cakes. Bess, the maiden aunt who had lived with Nettie, looked around the room and said to my mother, "Is there anything you would like to have from the house before we break it up?"

"No, I don't think so," Mother replied. She thought a minute and then added, "But I would like to have Father's letters."

"Really?" said Bess. "I'll get them right now."

Off she went up to the attic, and soon came down with a dusty shoe box full of letters.

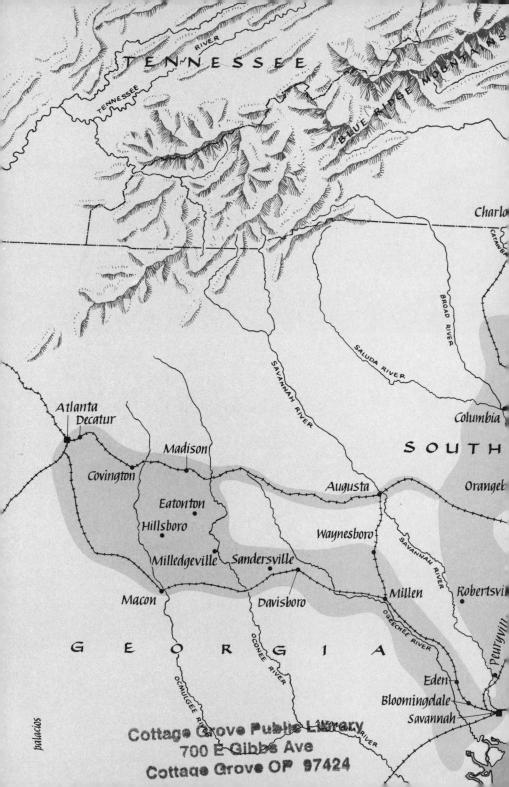

TENNESSEE

RIVER

TENNESSEE

BLUE RIDGE MOUNTAINS

Charlo

CATAWBA R.

BROAD RIVER

SALUDA RIVER

SAVANNAH RIVER

S O U T H

Columbia

Atlanta
Decatur

Madison

Covington

Augusta

Orangeb

Eatonton

Waynesboro

Hillsboro

SAVANNAH RIVER

Milledgeville Sandersville

Macon

Davisboro

Millen

Robertsvi

OGEECHEE RIVER

Peutyvill

G E O R G I A

OCONEE RIVER

Eden

Bloomingdale

OCMULGEE RIVER

Savannah

RIVER

palacios

Cottage Grove Public Library
700 E Gibbs Ave
Cottage Grove OR 97424